Rachaele Hambleton, aka Part-Time Working Mummy, is a double *Sunday Times* bestselling author and one of the most popular parenting personalities online. She is a mum to three daughters and one toddler son, step-mum to two boys and is married to her 'bird-boy' Josh. Her successful blog documents the highs and lows of life as a family of eight . . . with a dog and some chickens thrown in for good measure. As well as blogging and bringing up six humans, Rachaele fights hard for awareness of domestic violence and is an ambassador for Kidscape and a patron of Trevi in Plymouth. In 2021, Rachaele opened Torbay's first women's centre, which is a safe hub to support women and children. She is trying to make the world a better place by creating a wonderful community of nearly 800,000 people who support and empower one another.

Follow Rachaele here:

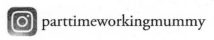 parttimeworkingmummy

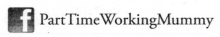 PartTimeWorkingMummy

Also by Rachaele Hambleton

Part-Time Working Mummy: A Patchwork Life
A Different Kind of Happy

THE PATCHWORK FAMILY

TODDLERS, TEENAGERS AND EVERYTHING IN BETWEEN

RACHAELE HAMBLETON

ROBINSON

ROBINSON

First published in Great Britain in 2023 by Robinson

1 3 5 7 9 10 8 6 4 2

A CIP catalogue record for this book
is available from the British Library.

ISBN: 978-1-47214-795-0

Typeset in Garamond by Hewer Text UK Ltd, Edinburgh
Printed and bound in Great Britain by Clays Ltd, Elcograf S.p.A.

Papers used by Robinson are from well-managed
forests and other responsible sources.

Robinson
An imprint of
Little, Brown Book Group
Carmelite House
50 Victoria Embankment
London EC4Y 0DZ

An Hachette UK Company
www.hachette.co.uk

www.littlebrown.co.uk

*To every woman who has walked through my women's
centre since 2021: thank you. Thank you for trusting
my team and me to support you. Your stories put
the fire in my belly to make the world a better place
for you and your babies. I promise that, for as long
as I am here, I won't ever stop fighting for you.*

CONTENTS

INTRODUCTION

Hi everyone . . . So, here we are again. I'm going to give myself a quick introduction here, just in case you've found this book in a leftover pile on holiday in your hotel (I can't tell you how many people have found me this way!), or perhaps you were given a copy by a friend who knows you might appreciate reading about the chaos that is my family life.

My name is Rachaele, I am forty (Jesus, I've only said that a few times since I turned forty recently and it sounds really strange . . . and feels even weirder).

I was born in Devon to a set of Mancunian parents who showed me pretty early on that mums and dads often get shit wrong (in many ways it destroyed me but in many ways it has bettered me as a parent and human and has given me the drive to do what I now do).

My parents separated when I was four; my mum left and moved to the other side of the country, I stayed with my dad. It all slowly fell apart (creating a lot of childhood trauma and rejection that I've been dealing with ever since). I went into foster care aged fifteen and then into my first bedsit at sixteen where I went off the rails fully for a good few years and survived on a diet that consisted mainly of class-A drugs, pasta and cheese and Blue WKD to numb the pain of some pretty fucking awful decisions I regularly made and rarely learnt from.

I now have four children by three men. Weirdly, my greatest achievement to date (no, seriously). I live in Torbay with my children – along with my husband and his two boys.

In our house there is no 'yours' and 'mine'. There's no 'step' or 'half'. We are just a crazy, huge, patchwork family, made up of lots of DNA, surnames and personalities, but it works better than most. I absolutely love it and actually I am beyond proud of everything we are and what we've achieved despite where we've come from.

My two eldest girls, Betsy, who is eighteen and Lula (short for Tallulah), who is thirteen, were born into a really unsafe household where they both lived with domestic abuse. I finally fled after almost a decade when the girls were almost seven and two.

I then had my third daughter, Edie. As I write this today she is nine, surrounded by love from her biological dad, who idolises her. Unfortunately, she was born at a time her dad and I were both pretty broken and, looking back,

I think we probably thought we could heal each other by getting together as we had been in a relationship at school many years before and thought the world of each other. We lost two babies in quick succession before Edie, which was soul-destroying for us both and a few months after she came along we separated. The split ended up being pretty brutal but nine years on things have got better, he loves her to bits and and vice versa.

I have a little boy, Wilby. He is three. He is the first and only child I have with my husband Josh who is/was/kind-of is (I'll explain properly later) a police officer. Josh has two other sons, Seb, aged sixteen, and Isaac, aged twelve. They were eight and four when we got together.

All in all we have six babies who live with us full time. Other than Edie – who sees her dad regularly – the other five are solely with us as a result of decisions by family court, and now they have no contact with their other biological parents.

It's complicated but it's a family full of love – and, let's face it, life is messy.

Back in 2016 I wrote a post that went viral on social media and then I started a blog to talk about real family life – because I didn't feel like I was seeing people like me. Where was the emotional baggage, the tears from a child being bullied, the daily trials and breaking points along with all the joy? I wanted to spread kindness and make people feel part of something bigger – you don't have to feel alone and excluded in darker times. Half a million people listened to me write about life as a blended family on Facebook. It seemed a lot of people were in agreement that life can be really fucking hard at times, but also pretty amazing too.

I now have a following of hundreds of thousands online as Part-Time Working Mummy (@parttimeworking-mummy on insta), have written two bestselling books and have set up women's centres to help those affected as I once was. It has been an incredible journey to this point – and the last five years since my first book have been absolutely life-changing.

In 2018, we had five tiny children aged between five and twelve. Now we have three, almost four teenagers, one of whom is an adult, along with a nine-year-old and we added another one to our flock because clearly we just weren't busy enough.

I mainly talk on Instagram Stories now, where I've gained almost a quarter of a million followers who under-line that life is one big rollercoaster that one day has you on your knees in tears and the next day has you jumping for joy.

Life is so strange when you actually sit and pick it apart. It takes a village to get you through it – but I've come to realise over the years that far too many people were given a shit hand in life and because of that they don't have a village; a lot of the time they don't have anyone. I try my best to create one online, because as lovely as the dusky pink, cream and rose gold Instagram accounts are, as amazing as it is to watch perfect marriages, well-behaved children and families living together in harmony, I promise, it isn't real life.

Some of the most damaged, broken and lonely people sit behind some of the most stunning Instagram pages you follow. The pages who fully have their shit together who you would give anything to be more like, sometimes they're the ones who are screaming inside to be saved . . . which is why my page is messy. It's crying until I laugh and laughing until I cry. It's teenagers making shit decisions, pre-teens copying them and toddlers teething, it's trying to navigate my way down the autism pathway for two of my babies. It's showing all kinds of humans how amazing they are but also how awful they can be. It's showing it's normal to fuck up and not be perfect. It's hormonal, it's heartbreaking but it's also happy.

It's just real life, in all its glory.

Why I'm writing this book

Right now I'm sat on a bench in the sun in Somerset, at the lodge I come to when I need some space to write. I come here always to plan and plot and work out exactly what I want to say, why and how.

This little wooden cabin is surrounded by nothing but trees and a fast-running river. I have birds and squirrels all around me; a huge dragonfly just whizzed past my head. There is no TV, no internet and no phone signal and it means for the next forty-eight hours I will do nothing but write, drink, eat and sleep. Josh will listen to downloaded podcasts on the Falklands War, bathe in the sun and cook the most incredible foods and, in the evenings, we will just hang out under blankets watching the stars next to the firepit, chatting about everything and nothing.

It's incredible – and a massive contrast to everyday life!

So, half a decade on from my first book, the family has grown, times have changed and many new lessons have been learned along the way. Writing helps me to make sense of it all.

As a quick overview:

We're still a crazy patchwork family, just a tiny bit bigger.

We're still living in Devon, but we moved house and bought our first home together.

I'm no longer working for the company I had been with for almost two decades. I left my employment just before my first book came out in 2018 to work full-time on social media, writing books and focusing on my dream of opening a women's centre.

Josh is kind of, but not currently, but still a police officer. He's just gone on a career break to be home more to support the kids and me, which is lush and I feel so fortunate that we are in a position to do this.

But I suppose all that matters is I'm still Rach, I'm still who I was then, even if it doesn't look like that. I still live for having a busy home full of animals, friends and kids who mainly don't belong to me, bustling with chaos and love and I still have the exact same hopes and dreams, and I never take for granted that in the last few years some of them have come true.

For the next few chapters I'm going to delve into my life a bit more, all the parts I no longer share on social media (because of the constant hateful shit from a small minority of anonymous people). I want to use this to reflect on the last five years, the ups and the downs and the lessons I've learned, and I hope you stick around to read it. And, if you do, I really hope it helps you in some way to see that, no matter how much we're all striving and working our arses off to get to 'that place' which just looks so perfect, to be 'that person' who has it all together, I want you to see that actually that place and that person doesn't really exist. Perfect people and perfect lives aren't real; we're all just plodding, winging it and hoping for the best and a lot of the time we get it wrong.

It doesn't matter how much money someone makes or inherits, how big their home is, how beautiful they look or well-behaved their kids are, we all have our struggles. I hope more than anything people come away from reading this book feeling better about themselves and wanting to be kind to others.

1

THE BEGINNINGS OF WILBY

I remember the day I found out I was pregnant with Wilby.

It was the end of November 2018.

I woke up, went to the bathroom and took a pregnancy test as I had every single day for the months beforehand when I wasn't on my period. I popped the test strip on the window sill of the bathroom and got in the shower. When I got out the shower, as I was drying my legs, I saw it was positive.

I never forget how it panned out. I couldn't contain my excitement so I ran from the bathroom into our bedroom, screaming Josh's name. (I'm still unsure why I was up and getting showered and he was still in bed as this is something that never happens!) He sat bolt upright and looked at the test result.

Now, we had had words a few weeks earlier about the amount of money I was spending on pregnancy tests and

I went on Amazon to bulk-buy a load of the cheap ones – instead of peeing directly on the stick you pee in a little pot then dip in a little test stick. I remember Josh questioning their accuracy and I could tell he didn't want me to get my hopes up in case it was not positive. I called our friend Lucy – I have no idea why I chose her, perhaps because she had conceived her babies through IVF. It had been soul-destroying for her at times but, as she was a health visitor, I knew she would be the person to tell a good from a shit pregnancy test when she saw one.

She giggled when I asked her and told me the chances of them being correct were 'probably high'. She advised me to go grab another test from the chemist to be sure, she then shouted 'Congratulations!' before hanging up.

I climbed back under the covers with Josh and we giggled like children at the 'what if' idea that it was really positive and we were actually having a baby!

I drove to the chemist after the school run, downing a bottle of water, then to the supermarket, downing a second bottle of water and bought three different brands of pregnancy tests. I went home and did them all in one piss which lasted about a minute and a half thanks to the amount of fluid I'd drunk. All three came up positive immediately.

I didn't want to get my hopes up but I was so excited deep down that I just couldn't stop smiling and talking to myself in a whisper. I always do that, thinking about it now;

if I'm happy or excited or upset or sad, I will genuinely whisper to myself the weirdest things. It's as if, whatever the feelings are, they are too intense not to talk to myself about them, like, 'Oh God, Rach, you are actually pregnant, this is just amazing' or, if I'm sad, 'Do not fucking cry again over it, you've got to get your shit together now.'

The only other time I talk to myself is when I'm on the toilet, pissed. That is the time in life I always like to give myself a full-on, rambling, pep talk. Always in a pub toilet too, having a full-blown chat with myself about everything that's gone wrong in life then reminding myself of my achievements, honestly. I wonder how many people talk to themselves, sober or pissed. Maybe I'll do an Instagram poll to find out.

Anyway, we booked an early scan privately. I just wanted to see a heartbeat as I had lost three babies before but, at six weeks, it was there, on a little black-and-white screen, flashing away. Weirdly it made me feel better, but the 'what if's were still niggling at me because of the miscarriages – and with two of them I had seen flashing heartbeats.

Morning sickness had started at about five weeks. I can't explain how shit I felt when people would say things like, 'Oh, it will pass.' I had never experienced anything like it with the girls' pregnancies and, as well as being physically sick after I had eaten any food, I would also gag and throw up at the weirdest thing. It was similar to being really hungover – my brain would punish me by thinking of things like an undercooked fried egg that had a jelly-like yolk, or I'd go past a fish-and-chip shop and just reading the specials board outside on the pavement would then make me picture fish and chips, which before this pregnancy I loved but now, imagining the picture of them in my head, covered in grease, was enough to make me vomit.

I also had days where I couldn't swallow – even swallowing my own spit made me sick. I remember Lula being the only one out of the kids happy enough to sit in the front seat of the car, holding a cake-mixing bowl on her lap on the way to school that she would lift up so I could spit in it as I drove.

There were waves – of knowing you were going to be sick, where you feel the sweat on the back of your neck and your hairs stand on end because you can't do anything to stop it coming. With that came the emotion, the genuine feeling of desperation because I could do nothing to make it go away, and this thing, this tiny, diddy thing growing inside me, no bigger than a strawberry – which was all I'd ever dreamed of – was making me feel more physically unwell than I'd ever been. Then came the guilt – because there were days I felt like I regretted getting pregnant, there were times I said to Josh out loud that I couldn't do it any more. It was honestly brutal.

I was prescribed medication by the GP, but I was still losing weight and I felt so weak and unwell. The only thing that got me through was sucking on boiled, sherbet lemon sweets, which – funnily enough – the thought of since having Wilby now themselves make me feel sick!

I accessed lots of pregnancy sickness support groups on Instagram when it started. The posts and comments from other pregnant women going through it made me feel I wasn't alone. And I was lucky, luckier than most, because at around fourteen weeks my symptoms started to ease, and by eighteen weeks I felt OK. Some women I met on the support pages had it for an entire nine months; they were hospitalised and put on drips because their weight loss and dehydration was so severe and they became so unwell that they needed to be constantly monitored by doctors. I genuinely don't know how they got through it and I feel that awareness of how bad it can be just isn't there – it wasn't for me until I experienced it. I honestly just thought morning sickness was morning sickness and how wrong I was.

I was also a wreck from worrying whether or not the pregnancy was going OK. I have never had a 'successful pregnancy' (a term I hate) without losing a baby first. I miscarried once between Betsy and Lula and I miscarried twice between Lula and Edie. I would spend those first few months flitting between feeling so excited I had butterflies, looking at prams and nursery furniture, to being in such a panic that I would miscarry, mentally planning how I would get through it when it happened.

I made the choice to announce finding out I was pregnant on Christmas Day 2018, before I had reached twelve weeks.

I remember the negative comments on my post about announcing too early, people thinking they had some kind of right to ask me why I hadn't waited until twelve weeks – until they said I was 'safe' to tell people – and it was so infuriating because it's so utterly wrong, the way society tells us how to do things. I was pregnant, I had all the feelings of excitement when I saw those test results, I was drowning in sickness and, actually, if I did lose my baby I know I wouldn't want to keep it a secret. Why should I keep it a secret? My page and the people who supported me had got me through so many bad times. I made a decision, if 'the worst' was to happen I would want to share that, to tell people, to hear their stories, listen to their words and know I wasn't alone. In turn, I knew from speaking about my earlier miscarriages that it had helped lots of other women, because so many of them lost babies every single day. We just don't see that as a society, because it's not talked about enough and the reason is the people wading in on my post giving it, 'Don't you think you should have waited until you hit twelve weeks and it's safe?'

No pregnancy is 'safe': women lose babies at four weeks, six weeks, sixteen weeks or full term. Women have babies born sleeping or who pass away after birth. There is never a 'safe time' and by pretending there is only makes things worse. It also makes it seem like a loss before twelve weeks is not a loss, like it's not something you have the right to grieve over or tell people because you weren't 'deemed safe'. It screams that you should keep something you're beyond excited about a secret for three months in case it doesn't pan out the way you dreamed it would. If the worst happens you should just 'crack on with it' rather than being able to feel like your heart has been ripped out and tell people you feel like your world has ended because society has already decided you're an idiot, having announced your pregnancy before you should have.

It's bullshit and I feel really angered for all the women who lose babies and have to break their hearts in private because of what 'society says'. I believe you announce when you want to announce, whether you're three weeks pregnant, three months or you don't feel like telling anyone at all. *The choice is yours*; don't allow anyone to make you feel you have to do things a certain way.

A different kind of pregnancy

I loved being pregnant, but the guilt I felt about Betsy and Tallulah was overwhelming at times. I thought about all the things they experienced whilst they grew inside me. Through both of their pregnancies there were regular arguments, screaming, shouting and violence. The police were called out to my home by neighbours. I battled daily in my own head about why I was having these babies in such shit circumstances and I would cry most days. I've since learned – and actually we now train this in our women's centres as part of our domestic abuse programme – that because domestic abuse raises a woman's stress levels, we produce a high level of the stress hormone cortisol. This enables our body to react to danger, which triggers our fight-or-flight mode. Some research has shown that there is a direct association between a mother's level of this hormone and those in an unborn baby.

When I got further into my pregnancy with Wilby and began to relax more, I realised how special it felt to be in a positive, healthy relationship where there was no screaming or shouting, no slamming of doors or throwing of objects. I wasn't getting dragged around or spat at. I realised how amazing it was for him, even though he wasn't even aware, that he had a daddy who loved him, who chatted to him through my belly and blew raspberries on my tummy until he kicked and who took incredible care of his mummy. I felt so fortunate, so grateful, because of what the two eldest girls and I had come from, to now, having this baby where we all felt loved, protected and cared for. With that realisation came the guilt that neither Betsy nor Lula had never had this – and Edie, to an extent because I wasn't myself whilst I was pregnant with her. Her dad worked away so much of the time and then we separated when she was tiny. I felt a guilt that none of them had ever had 'this mummy' that Wilby already had. None of my girls had ever had this version of me, not really, and that made me feel really shit at times; it still does today. Having Wilby made me know I would never take for granted the surroundings he developed in and I felt grateful every day for the life he would have, the constant love he would receive, and the lives his brothers and sisters now had.

I put on a lot of weight during my pregnancy, mainly on my bum and bump! I was bigger than I had been with the girls and I struggled with backache really badly. I saw a chiropractor called Phoebe who was amazing and pulled and tugged at me most weeks, which helped me manage the pain. At a midwife appointment when I was around thirty weeks, she tested my urine and was concerned about the reading. She sent me immediately to Torbay hospital to be tested for gestational diabetes, which came back positive. I remember feeling really ashamed and embarrassed, feeling that it was my fault because, although I ate a good lunch and dinner full of fresh veg, I worried my love of double cream on cornflakes in the morning and a can of full-fat Coke with every evening meal had caused this. This was because society has always portrayed a bad diet as leading to a diagnosis of diabetes. Ridiculous, and upsetting in hindsight for me, but also for the people living with diabetes who have to see the memes on the internet I often saw which blame your diet and greed – it's not the case in a lot of cases.

I was then told my baby was likely to be 'overweight', as the scans were currently showing him or her being 'bigger' than they should have been. This meant I would need to have another caesarean because the risks were too high to have a vaginal delivery. I felt awful. The reality, which I learned after having a meeting with the diabetes nurse, is that during pregnancy your placenta makes hormones that cause glucose to build up in your blood. Usually, your pancreas can send out enough insulin to handle it. But if your body can't make enough insulin or stops using insulin as it should, your blood-sugar levels rise, and you get gestational diabetes.

I had to prick my finger three times a day then test my sugar levels; it was quick and easy to do and there's an app to log your test results on so you can liaise with the hospital to manage your levels with diet or medication.

As soon as Wilby was born we were both tested and, just as they said, the diabetes had immediately disappeared and his levels were fine within forty-eight hours of being born. The chances of me getting diabetes in life are now higher, and more likely in future pregnancies, but it was a condition I found manageable. At the time I didn't feel like I could share online and I only told close friends and family – I didn't have any awareness of the condition and I felt a bit of shame and worry around it. Hopefully writing about it here will help some other people.

2

WILBY'S BIRTH

We didn't find out the sex of the baby; neither of us wanted to. I was convinced it was a girl, because I'd only ever had girls. Josh didn't have a gut feeling on either sex – one week he said 'boy' and one week he said 'girl'! As many people said, 'It's definitely a girl' as the ones who said 'That's a boy bump'; we just had to wait. We got a red pram and everything else was neutral or rainbow-themed.

We were scanned weekly due to the diabetes and by week thirty-six Wilby was weighing in at around nine pounds so we made the decision to have an elective C-section. All the girls had been between 6-lb 13-oz and 7-lb 10-oz so I remember feeling really worried.

I was seriously gutted about having to go for a caesarean because we had done a hypnobirthing course and it honestly changed my entire views on pregnancy and giving birth.

I had heard hypnobirthing being raved about on Instagram and I really wanted a home birth. Josh was totally against it, as were many other family members, telling me it was dangerous and would put both the baby and me at too much unnecessary risk. I decided to contact a local girl called Siobhan who runs a company called Positive Hypnobirthing. I asked her a few questions and she offered to meet me for a coffee.

I went to a cafe in Newton Abbot, where we chatted about everything and nothing and instantly I really liked her. Her voice alone was really calming and she just had a way of making you feel at ease. I signed Josh and me up to do her course, which ran in one of the rooms at the local birth suite. Josh wasn't overly keen – he doesn't really do humans at the best of times and I could tell he felt like it would be really uncomfortable. His words when I told him were, 'I just don't feel like rolling round on birth balls rubbing your belly, Rach, whilst we both pant in harmony in front of a room full of strangers.' It made me giggle and, as much as I was slightly cringing at not knowing what I had signed us up to, I liked Siobhan and I had a good feeling.

The course ran over two days, and Josh was sold two hours in; we couldn't have been more wrong about what it entailed. I was so gutted I had gone through three pregnancies, labours and births without knowing about the stuff we were taught – simple facts that you have no clue about because you think you have to hand yourself and your body over to midwives and doctors because 'they know best'.

There were simple changes of words or sentences like swapping 'contractions' (which sound horrid and painful) to 'surges' (which sound powerful and strong) and the stats behind the higher number of women who go into distress in hospital birthing units as opposed to home births and the reasoning behind this. I learned so much about my body and why I could have had such nicer, better informed previous births with the girls, stuff that seemed so simple and obvious once it had been pointed out to us. That's something else hypnobirthing taught me; until I did that course no one had ever just pointed out the obvious. It was honestly mind-blowing and made both Josh and me really emotional and excited about going into labour and meeting our baby. I had never got excited about having a baby; in fact the three times before this I had dreaded giving birth and been feeling nothing but panic and anxiety, but hypnobirthing gives you tools to manage pain, it gives your birth partner a role and it makes one of the most magical things in your life feel positive instead of totally terrifying!

By then Josh wanted the home birth as much as me. We began looking into the best ways to do it and he found a local pool-hire company, called and popped a deposit down. We were buzzing about it all until the news came I had gestational diabetes and it would medically be danger-ous to not have a caesarean section. I felt like all our dreams had been shattered but another amazing thing with hypnobirthing is it allows you to see you have control over your own body and it gives you the confidence to question medical staff's decisions and ensure your views and opinions are heard even if you have to change your plans because of medical reasons.

We opted for a 'natural C-section' which we were lucky that they offer at Torbay hospital. Six years earlier, I had a very structured, quick-as-possible operation in an extremely clinical setting with Edie, when she was pulled out by a team of people in scrubs who didn't talk to me much. She was immediately taken away and cleaned whilst I was stitched back up before I met her. This time I could have the lighting dimmed so it felt cosier, I could have my own music playing and the whole medical team were really relaxed, chatty and actually fun. They made me feel at ease and we were having a laugh about stuff beforehand.

The surgeon then made the incision and they allowed the baby to make his own way out, which was less stressful for him. The curtain was also lowered during the opera-tion and I could watch the whole process happening. It was insane: I watched my baby wriggle out of my belly then crawl upwards towards my face before the surgeon scooped him up and Josh wailed, 'It's a little boy.'

The baby was then placed upon my chest, where he gripped onto one of Josh's fingers and one of mine as tight as he could! The three of us had a little cry together and, as the team worked on stitching my tummy up, I felt like I'd won the lottery. He weighed in at a whopping 9-lb 4-oz and had a mop of jet-black hair and a perfect, heart-shaped birthmark which sat really prominently on his forehead. He was just incredible and I can't even describe how much more meeting him made me fall head over heels in love with his daddy all over again.

Josh and I went back to our room on the ward below the labour suite and snuggled our little boy together. I latched him on to feed and he suckled away at me like a baby piglet. That feeling: it's inexplicable. The utter pain your body is in from using every part of you to deliver this miracle, the exhaustion you feel from it all, but the elation, that feeling where you just wipe away tears of sheer happiness is something else, and having a husband who did the same alongside me was the best feeling ever.

I remember when I breastfed, for months after, Josh would get really emotional and when I asked why he would just say, 'He's just so perfect and you're such a good mum.'

I'd never experienced having a partner who recognised how fucking hard and exhausting it was and who so openly showed his appreciation to me as his little boy's mum. I spent hours watching him gaze at Wilby, watching him study his tiny fingers or changing his nappy.

We stayed in hospital for two nights as I had a few minor complications with being unable to pee after the catheter was removed. Josh brought all five kids up to see me a few hours after Wilby was born. We had a long list of names which I had saved on my phone that we had all picked; I really wanted them to be a part of everything about their new brother. When they arrived their little faces made me sob. Betsy started crying as soon as she laid eyes on him and Edie just couldn't cope with how tiny he was. They passed him round the room whilst sniffing him and snuggling him loads.

I asked them what name we should have and we went through the list. The only one we all kind of liked was one Josh had chosen – Willoughby. He had picked it after a man called Willoughby Verner, an ornithologist born in 1852. We didn't like the whole name but we all liked something about it, so we played about with it and, between the seven of us, we came up with the name 'Wilby'. We all agreed and named him together in the hospital room. As soon as I managed to have a wee the following day the delivery team agreed I could go home and they discharged me. Josh packed up our bags and we took our new baby home to hang out with his big brothers and sisters.

At home with our new baby boy

For the next few months, when Josh wasn't working, he was at home, doing whatever needed doing in the background so the only thing I had to concentrate on was caring for Wilby. It was something else that was alien to me: a partner who did more than their fair share because they could see they just had to for a while. And there was no resentment that he had to do that, he just did it without question.

Wilby had colic quite early on and would scream and scream every day. He was at his worst every evening between 4 and 7 p.m. I remember Josh was so patient with him; he would just rock him in his arms and walk with him round the house for hours. He never got upset or stressed or annoyed, he just loved him. Wilby would only settle when Josh was moving.

I think maybe the smell of breastmilk from me would upset him more as he would try and feed but then he would scream more, like an angry cry, like he was in such pain. We quickly worked out he was best with Josh when he had these unsettled periods. This meant I got a few hours to hang out with the older kids and do some bits round the house. We would then swap roles when Wilby calmed and I would spend evenings on the sofa with him cluster-feeding on me whilst Josh finished up, put the kids to bed and got them ready for the next day with ironed shirts and packed lunches, always happily doing it. Whenever I would say I felt bad or guilty because I spent all my time caring for Wilby he told me how much he loved seeing him so content feeding and I loved it too.

I loved for the first time just being able to be a mum over and above anything else. I loved being able to soak up the first six months of my newborn without that underlying guilt that had been drilled into me from having the girls that I wasn't 'doing enough', 'pulling my weight' round the house, 'earning any money' or not 'making an effort' with myself.

Whatever other shit was happening in my life, my home still felt like a little safe place and my babies continued to help fix all my bits that felt really broken at that time.

When the world changed

Coronavirus swept the world in 2020. I remember there was loads going on when the talk of lockdown first began in March.

I was in London the week before, working on a campaign with some other content creators. I remember it all feeling really weird and surreal, like we didn't know what was to come because everyone was carrying on with life, trying to pretend things were still normal.

I look back and remember we were at a Lewis Capaldi concert surrounded by tens of thousands of people at Wembley Arena then a week later we were on lockdown in our house. It was insane.

Tallulah had just been to Nottingham with my niece to stay with my friend Gayle and I took Betsy shopping for a prom dress which was scheduled for the July.

Within a few weeks, we went into the national lockdown; our freedom disappeared overnight and was replaced by strict rules and regulations. I remember it feeling really frightening.

Josh was in a role which meant luckily he could work from home. He set up an office in our middle lounge where he would work his shifts. I remember he had the news on in there all day in the background. Listening to the forecast of expected deaths, the rush of temporary hospitals being built to cope with what was to come, the threats of what would happen if we mixed with relatives or friends. It felt really scary. I watched one news episode on TV where the reporters were in a block of flats in Bristol, speaking to a single dad and his son at the time we weren't allowed to go outside. They had no garden and he couldn't afford to pay for the internet to home school or keep his son entertained. Watching the dad trying to stay positive despite such uncertainty, when I could just see the look of worry in his eyes and his little boy who had no real understanding of how his world had overnight turned upside down, just broke me. I felt so lucky to be in the position we were in, for Josh and me to still be employed and earning and the fact we had a secure home and a large garden for the kids. I remember just feeling so safe; despite us not being able to leave the house or see anyone we were together, the eight of us, and it was something I never wanted to take for granted. I wondered how I could do more to help people like that dad.

I stopped watching the news, the death tolls, the constant updates and warnings we were all getting about what would happen if we left the house unnecessarily. The reports of people dying alone in hospital and others unable to attend funerals of loved ones. It just made me feel so anxious and worried and it was something I couldn't control or stop. I decided to focus on what we could do.

It even felt frightening to go to the supermarket in case we caught Covid-19. Everyone was so frightened of this unknown illness and the media hype that surrounded it felt so weird. We began getting doorstep deliveries of our food. Josh and I would go in the porch and wipe it all with anti-bac whilst wearing gloves before we brought it in.

Cooking became a huge part of our day because we weren't leaving the house. We would plan recipes and Josh would make the most fabulous meals. At this point Wilby had just weaned and he loved his food so we made all kinds of puréed dishes for him too. We would eat together three times a day, all of us and it felt like we properly bonded again as a family. I suppose before Covid, because the kids were bigger, they were at different clubs and were at friends' houses. Isaac spent a few nights at Josh's mum's or sister's each week. It wasn't often we all sat and ate dinner together any more, and it was only when we were forced to do so because of a global pandemic I realised how important it was, and how much I had missed it – us all being together, sharing stories, having banter where we laughed until we cried and we just learned so much about each other's thoughts and opinions on the most random stuff.

In all honesty, Josh and I both say we loved that first lockdown period. He was home with us, we were all together and we spent time enjoying the simplest stuff that we had forgotten was so special. We also all got to spend time with Wilby, who was seven months old and just starting to be interested in all of us and his surroundings. Having his brothers and sisters with him every day as well as me and Josh felt really magical to watch.

A woman and a fridge

I realised at this point that there were so many families who weren't like ours. I imagined how I would have tried to navigate my way through this period if it had happened twelve years ago, when I was alone in a horrid flat with Betsy and Lula with nothing and it knocked me sick. I needed to do more to help; I was in a position where it would have felt wrong not to do something.

I received an email from a lady called Nina who worked for a local community interest company and was desperate to raise its community fridge profile. I was just blown away by what she was doing for others and our community. The way her community fridge worked was she would drive round to supermarkets and collect their 'waste food'. She was passionate about the planet and not allowing food to be binned. She would do 'open days' at one of the centres she worked at, where any member of the public could come and collect the food twice a week. I began volunteering for her immediately. What I loved was that she made this about people helping themselves and the planet, which was how it should be. It was never about people feeling they had to live in poverty or on benefits to access the service. It never sat right with me that certain food banks make you evidence how you are struggling so much financially that you need to collect a food parcel. I know how ashamed and embarrassed I was when I lived in poverty after having the girls – and actually, on paper I had a well-paid managerial role and didn't qualify for most benefits. Nowadays I probably wouldn't have qualified to access a food bank but the reality was that I was drowning in the debt the eldest girls' dad had left me and I couldn't afford to feed my children some weeks.

Covid had done something similar to so many families. Families that had been wealthy had their whole lives turned upside down overnight when their successful businesses had gone under, but they wouldn't have been able to access certain food banks because they weren't claiming benefits, so to have them come to what Nina had created and collect all sorts of weird and wonderful food that they could use was really heartwarming.

She took whatever was there at the supermarket when she arrived for the collections – some nights there would be just a few packs of ham or loaves of bread and some nights Nina would have to go back several times and re-fill her car again and again because there was so much. Nina was adamant no food would go to waste; what people didn't take was cooked and frozen. She delivered meals she made every Friday to elderly vulnerable people within our community too. Betsy and I took it in turns to go along with her and we both sobbed at how devastating it was to see the way some elderly people are left to live. Some had mobility or health issues and were housed in the most inappropriate places – in flats up steep concrete steps, in homes that were filthy and in a poor state of repair. All that these old men and ladies really wanted was our time; they wanted us to sit and chat to them, and it was always about us. These people would ask me questions about my children, my job, my interests, but they rarely spoke of themselves.

I used to get back in the car and start to cry and Nina would say, 'I know, Rach, it's absolutely brutal.' And it was. And it is something that is not seen. There is no awareness until it smacks you in the face. I'd never realised how high was the number of elderly people who actually are as vulnerable as small children a lot of the time, living minutes from my house, within my community, in places where I wouldn't house a dog.

Nina would make the most incredible curries or roast dinners. She would make delicious bread-and-butter puddings out of the loaves of bread that were left over, while the weird vegetables would go into homemade soups or sauces for pasta dishes. She filled fridges and freezers full of her meals which she would then drive over to Shaldon zoo, Teignmouth, for the keepers to feed to the animals.

There was so much Nina taught me in those few months and there was so much of it I really loved. I loved how she had a passion; she was just so passionate about food wastage and helping others, but she did it in a way that left me in awe of her because she saw people, she saw everyone – whether it was an electrician without much work because of Covid who was panicking about his future or if it was a heroin addict who turned up on a Saturday with her kids dressed in school uniform because they had no other clothes. Nina just saw them and she had a way of seeing the bigger picture without judging. Even those who were judged by other people, she knew all about cycles and history repeating itself and why so many of these people we were supporting didn't know how to live any other way. She spoke to everyone in a way that was tailored to them, to show she had a genuine interest and to see what she could do to help them as individuals with their own needs. She got some men's toiletries for the electrician and we got together a huge bag of clothes and toys for the children of the lady living with addiction and we did this for anyone who needed specific clothes, household items or foods. Anyone and everyone, we just did simple things together, to make their lives a little bit easier and I suppose to show them that someone cared.

She also taught me about community – about how so many people will help, they want to help, but often they don't know how. It worked well, because she had the knowledge and I had the platform on social media, so between us we managed to raise the awareness of what was needed locally to help others and we achieved incredible things.

People volunteered their time to come in and man the community fridge or sort through donations. People also made donations – food and then presents for kids for Christmas. It was so amazing to see and be a part of and every time I came home I just felt incredibly emotional and I had this buzz which made me feel so high and happy from helping other people and seeing, but also knowing because of my own experiences, what that would have meant and done for them.

Nina definitely made me want to do something more to help others. She made me see how lives could be changed by something so simple as giving away food without question or judgement or coordinating donations and then getting them out to the people who needed them. It made me see that actually this was something I had to make happen too.

The lows of lockdown

We continued at home as a family through lockdown, but when those first few weeks turned to months, it began having a real impact on all the kids, mainly Betsy and Seb. Betsy had all her GSCEs cancelled and came down with symptoms of Covid on her last day of school. I kept her off against her will but the test result then came back negative the following day and I remember her anger, her crying that she hadn't been part of the day as she watched her friends all over social media sign each other's shirts and just be at one of the most memorable important times for a teenager. Their prom was cancelled after we had bought her dress. Her boyfriend also ended their year-long – and her first serious – relationship. She was broken.

I remember it being one of the first times of realising, as a parent, that some things your babies go through you just can't heal. When they're tiny and they fall and cut their knees, get upset after having a bad dream or argue with their best friend over a sticker pack at school you can calm them down, reassure them it will be OK. You can feed them ice cream, snuggle them on the sofa under a blanket and the world quickly becomes brighter again, but at this point with Betsy I just couldn't make her better. I couldn't make anything feel any better because I couldn't re-open her school so she could see her friends, I couldn't book her hair and makeup and pay towards a limo and demand her prom went ahead like all the proms she'd watched on social media at her school all the years before hers and I couldn't make her ex-boyfriend change his mind and go back to how it was before he decided he didn't want to be in a relationship with her.

All I could do was love her and promise her it was all temporary, everything is temporary . . . but it was hard, she was full of every emotion and being stuck in the house with nothing to occupy her mind or give her a focus was torture. She had a mattress on the floor of my room where she slept for weeks and in the middle of the night I would just hear her silent sobs. I would sneak in next to her and wrap her into me, kissing her forehead repeatedly, stroking her hair and her arms whilst repeating, 'It's all gonna be OK, baby,' and I just felt her body heave with silent sobs and felt her tears running down my arm and chest and it hurt, it hurt like a physical pain inside me that I couldn't make disappear. I would have given anything at that point to rewind time, take her back to being a little girl when, no matter how bad things were, I could fix them with an arm tickle and a tub of ice cream.

I knew how bad she felt, because I had been her age, going through similar stuff and it feels like your world is ending, but on top of this she was living at a time when Covid had made it unrecognisably hard for all of us too. That stress, pressure and confusion was weighing so heavy on her and she desperately needed to return to normal.

At the same time, Seb was massively struggling. He was used to going all over the country with his friends scooter-riding. As soon as he finished school in the afternoons and every weekend and school holidays he would be at a skate park. He and his friends would get on the train on a Saturday morning and go to Cardiff or Corby, learning the most amazing scooter tricks and just having fun. Now he was only allowed out for an hour a day to exercise and the skate park was closed and taped up. After a while his mates started going there again and riding, but you weren't allowed to 'meet people' and we constantly had to tell him about breaking rules. Rules which were just so unfair to a teenage boy who was watching all his mates doing what he was desperate to do. Rules that made Josh and me feel utterly shit for having to constantly implement. The guilt I felt that we had to refuse to let him do stuff he loved and had always done whilst reassuring him it was to keep 'him and others safe' but he was watching other people do it and they appeared perfectly safe. It just felt so cruel and unfair for both the kids and there were times I often worried about the long-term effects Covid would have on them.

Isaac and Lula both coped really well with lockdown. At this point, Lula hated school and had never had a friendship circle so was happy to be at home and Isaac was still at primary and hadn't begun going out and meeting friends out of hours. He was also fine with being at home. Edie struggled with not being able to go out and do stuff with us like she was used to and for her it was difficult because she had no understanding of why we couldn't do it, but she was allowed to go between her dad's and our house so that respite, change of scenery and transition helped to keep her happy, I think.

We then went through that period of coming out of lockdown, before going back under and having certain restrictions one day but not the next. It frustrated me as an adult with a level of understanding so for my children it was utterly exhausting and made them so angry.

We had to be particularly careful because we are well-known due to our internet profile. Josh has said that my job is no different to his. As a police officer there are certain expectations on you to do stuff and to not do stuff and it was now the same for me – if not worse – because cancel culture, as we repeatedly see, is real. If we weren't sure of something it just couldn't happen. If Betsy and

Seb's friends were all doing something we weren't a hundred per cent sure was allowed, we couldn't allow them to go – because the risk was too great. If we did get it wrong and someone filmed them or took a picture and posted it on social media or sent it to Josh's employers, we could get into trouble. A lot of the time we stopped them doing stuff they were allowed to do, just because so many people still had the opinion it was wrong because of Covid. I'm annoyed at myself now, looking back, that I did that to them, because there were days I kept them home whilst their friends met up and they'd be distraught they weren't allowed to join in, but it was terrifying. It was so unknown, overwhelming and scary. They really struggled with one day being able to do something that the next day they couldn't. We lived under a constant black cloud of having to put a hold on planning anything in case we were back in lockdown.

For example, when Josh was working, he took a picture of a takeaway coffee on his Instagram while he was on shift and tagged the coffee shop on Instagram to give their little struggling business a boost. Within days, our fears were confirmed when his work called him to say they had received anonymous allegations and complaints that he had broken the law by being out of his area without reason. He hadn't and he wasn't, but I knew then we were being watched, the kids were being watched – properly watched – and I knew I needed to continue to be hot on all the rule changes as and when they happened. It was so hard. There were rows, huge rows. Their friends continued to do everything they wanted to do and the kids knew they had good parents too yet they were still allowed. They decided Josh and I were the shit parents who were out to ruin their lives, they hated Josh being a police officer and they hated me being on the internet – and a lot of the time it felt like they really hated us. I remember the last few months of it all feeling hard, long and emotionally-fucking-draining.

My work went crazy during lockdown, because so many people were at home, still being paid, with nothing to do and I had brand after brand contact me to offer me various campaign deals. For so many, lockdown was a devastating time financially, but for me it was a time when I managed to earn enough money to know that, once Covid was behind us, I would have a lump sum large enough to fulfil my dreams of opening a women's centre locally. There was the rise of domestic abuse and I worked with campaigns during lockdown such as Rail To Refuge (offering free train travel for those fleeing abuse) with charities like Women's Aid and Refuge. It would be desperately needed more than ever.

We also had to home school. For Lula and Seb, it was quite easy because they logged on and did their own thing but Isaac and Edie were at primary and they got different subjects set on all kinds of platforms. Some of the work wasn't compatible with Edie's iPad so she would complete it then it would just disappear. I would then get an email asking why she wasn't doing it and she would get so frustrated and I would get frustrated. Seb and Lula skipped lessons – again I would get emails – and Betsy spent her time attempting to revise for exams she never ended up taking. It was hard.

On the days Josh wasn't working I remember him just nailing it. He would get them up, feed them and then set up two work stations – one in the kitchen and one in the green lounge. He would support Seb and Lula to join their lessons and ensure they had everything they needed to get started. He would then sit with Edie and Isaac and help them do everything they needed to do. He would implement breaks where he would give them a snack and drink, he would get them all doing the Joe Wicks PE challenge in the middle lounge and then they'd finish for the day. He ordered extra learning books from Amazon that they worked through and completed when they had a quiet school learning day. When Edie lost her mind and couldn't do the work because of the iPad playing up he calmly called the school and explained what was happening. One of the teachers lived close to us and was still teaching at the school during this time so she delivered Edie's work in paper form each week to our porch and we left her completed work there the next week for her to take away. He just made it work with them all with ease whilst I cared for Wilby. I would then start work in our room where I would dissect contracts, briefs and film adverts once the 'school day' was over and Josh could watch Wilby and the others would chill out round the house.

The problem was that when Josh was working, the middle lounge was out of bounds as that's where he based himself and his work needed to be confidential and quiet – and having all six of them in the kitchen didn't work. I would let a few go to their rooms and trust them to work, but they didn't. I was also caring for a breastfeeding baby who was really demanding a lot of the time and, to be honest, I just didn't get the school work. I am beyond crap at maths and geography. It was like my brain reverted back to the last few years I was at school and every time they asked me for help with a question I froze and felt instantly overwhelmed.

I just felt like I was drowning and I kept seeing all these mums on Instagram who had set up the cutest work stations for their kids and were absolutely loving home schooling, had nailed a brilliant routine, everyone was sat together getting on and it looked perfect.

I remember one day I called Josh's sister in tears. Her son is the same age as Isaac and he, like Isaac, was struggling with the home learning. I remember her answering the phone and I was just wailing to her about how I was a shit mum and I couldn't do it any more. I never forget her response, 'Well, Alfie and I had a row this morning because he's just refusing to do anything so I left him sat at the computer and went in the kitchen. He thought it would be a good idea to secretly type "FUCK OFF" in a rage in capital letters on the keyboard so it came up on the screen for him to see but he accidentally sent it in to the group chat, so his teachers contacted me asking what the reason was that all the kids in his class, and their parents, have just read that from him.'

I went from crying to hysterically laughing, because it was the first time I had thought about it from the kids' point of view and how hard this shit situation was for most of them. To have their entire lives go upside down and back to front overnight. They were used to spending their days with structure and routine whilst they were surrounded by hundreds of other children and their best friends and now they were isolated, with just their parents or caregivers and annoying siblings in front of a weird screen trying to do work that a lot of the time they didn't understand and nor did the person trying their best to support them. It was just so fucked up for everyone. So mentally hard and draining. And that was for the kids who lived in safe, secure homes where they were loved. I began to think how it must have been for the children whose only safe space was school. Horrific.

That day I thought, Fuck it. I remember sitting in my room on my Instagram Stories and just being honest. Honest that I fucking hated home schooling, that I was arguing with my kids constantly and far too much with Josh. I felt so angry but I didn't know who with or particularly why. I was just mentally struggling and actually being locked down in a house with six children in a situation that was alien to us all was taking its toll. I spoke about hating the parent I was being. I didn't like being the mum that got frustrated at my kids' frustrations when they had every right to feel frustrated. I hated that I was snappy and short-tempered with them all. I hated everything at that point and I'd had enough. It was just too much.

The response I had was mind-blowing. I think 90 per cent of my followers felt the same. Even the ones who stayed home all day and had grid pictures of their home school set-ups or messy play corners they'd created for their babies. The ones who were still going out to work and leaving their children behind in such uncertain times. Everyone was battling and struggling, no matter what their situation was and it was a reminder to me yet again that a lot of the time, nothing is ever as perfect as it looks on social media. Everyone you meet has their own kind of issues behind closed doors, even if they're not visible to us on the outside.

3

THE PALM TREE YEARS

The world started to return to normal in summer 2021.

During lockdown, when I was struggling to juggle everything, I started Wilby at a nursery so I could better support the big children with home schooling and work. I had been feeling guilty I was working because I was having to get the kids to entertain Wilby.

He went to a nursery close to us that was really lovely and a few of my friends' kids went there and they raved about it. We weren't allowed to stay to settle him because of Covid so I had to hand him over at the door to a nursery worker who was wearing a visor and a mask. He was petrified.

He had a one-hour settling-in session to begin with. During that time, they told me he didn't calm at all. It was the same the second time, but literally as soon as I parked: he knew where we were immediately which I found really odd. They said that it was normal for children to get upset but usually they will calm, even if just for a few seconds, to nosey at other children or their surroundings. They will then remember where they are and cry again, but this gets easier and better with each visit. Wilby didn't calm once and was gagging like he was going to be sick because he was getting himself in such a state.

The nursery was happy to keep trying but they kept me updated with how things were going. Both times I collected him he was dripping with sweat, gasping for breath from crying and he continued doing those little sobs for hours after he calmed down, even in his sleep. The third time I went to take him he began crying as soon as he saw the nursery sign. It was a panicky cry like he was frightened – he then went into a full-blown meltdown. I pulled the car up outside, but by the time I had got out of my seat and around to his door he was covered in sick because he had got so overwhelmed. I got him out and cuddled him but couldn't calm him down; he was worsening and totally inconsolable.

I rang the nursery and said, 'I'm outside with Wilby.'

The worker said, 'We can hear you,' and we both did a little laugh, that immediately turned to tears for me. I said I didn't know what to do.

Due to Covid restrictions she couldn't come and assist me as we still had to social-distance. She was asking what I wanted to do but I could hardly hear her because Wilby was crying uncontrollably. He threw up again, over us both and I knew he wasn't going to calm down whilst we continued to stand outside the place that was making him feel like this because I was quickly realising he had the most extraordinary memory for a small baby and he knew exactly where we were. I had no choice but to put him in his car seat and drive us home, both of us sobbing and covered in sick.

I walked through the front door and I just felt done. Josh scooped us both up, got Wilby bathed and settled and reassured me that we would manage the childcare between us without Wilby going to nursery. But this was something I knew deep down, with both our jobs, and how demanding they were, it was impossible. It just felt tough, and unknown, because all five of the others had gone to nursery or a childminder with just a few teething problems whilst they first settled – nothing like this. Again, I put it down to Wilby being a lockdown baby and in my head I convinced myself Josh was right and we would just have to manage the childcare between us.

The effect lockdown had on Wilby became more apparent when we started going out with him when the restrictions eased. He had been just seven months old when we went into full lockdown and he was now almost two years old.

To start with he was non-verbal. I remembered all the others were saying full sentences by this point. Still, I reminded myself he was the youngest of six siblings who all spoke for him. I remember the first day we took him out and, when a car drove past us, his whole body shook and he flapped his arms. His head spun to follow the sound he could hear and I could feel his heart banging out of his chest against mine. I felt sad that something so normal was completely alien to him; he had missed out on a huge chunk of time that, developmentally, was crucial.

Josh began taking Wilby to the bottom of our drive each day to get him used to the cars driving past but he would continue to shake, flap his hands and make loud screeching noises every time a car went past for months. He had done the same since he was tiny at certain TV programmes he liked so we decided he just loved cars and they made him happy. But the more stuff we did with him in public the more we noticed it happening. Simple things like a palm tree or some cow statues in our local park would make him have the same reactions. He would stand at them and just squeal, giggle, make loud noises, flap his arms and his body would tremble. Sometimes I couldn't work out if he was frightened or happy from the noises he made and facial expressions he pulled and his body language; it was just so overwhelming for him. The whole time his entire body would shake and he would flap his arms with his fingers either wide apart and rigid or his fists clenched so tightly his hands turned white. He would stand high on his tiptoes. I loved how he loved such simple stuff. The others had never been anything like this.

The bad part was when we tried to leave the areas he loved. He couldn't cope at all when we walked away from things like the palm tree or the cows or anything else he was overwhelmed by. He would have what I thought at the time was a full-blown tantrum. There was nothing other than lockdown I blamed this for: the fact he had spent fourteen months in a house instead of going out and exploring the world as his brothers and sisters had.

What went from him shouting and crying when we left a certain area quickly turned into him attacking Josh or me and if we put him down to stop him being violent, he would hurl himself on the floor and smash his head off any surface – concrete, gravel – nothing stopped him. It was like he couldn't feel pain. Within a matter of months of lockdown being over I wouldn't take him out without Josh or Betsy. I couldn't physically or emotionally manage his meltdowns in public. He was so loud, I have honestly never heard a baby cry and scream like him, probably because he's mine – but the stares I got from strangers in the street, watching me try and wrestle a toddler who appeared to be physically stronger than me, who I clearly had no control over, was soul-destroying.

When I met Josh all those years ago, I would take Seb all over Devon playing football on a Sunday morning whilst he worked. I had five children aged between eight months and ten years old who I could take care of with ease. We'd be out of the house all day, they'd behave on a football sideline in any weather, yet now I couldn't manage one child out the house alone. I honestly fucking hated lockdown.

I didn't have many friends with toddlers the same age at this point. One day Josh and I took Wilby to our local park. There was a little boy there who looked around the same age as him. I remember feeling really worried, as Wilby hadn't mixed with any other children his age, he had never shown any interest and as the little boy came over to play with Wilby I explained to his mum he wasn't used to children his age. I was so anxious about how he would behave and I constantly ran the worst scenario in my head. Looking back, I remember just being full of fear whenever we were out in public anywhere. And as I'd imagined, Wilby immediately smacked the boy in the face and I wanted to cry. The mum reassured me it was fine and her little boy threw sand back at Wilby in retaliation. I ended up chatting to her; she was called Dani and her little boy was called Isaac. He was a few months older than Wilby. I instantly liked her, she reminded me of me. The me before people on the internet had destroyed my self-confidence and made me question everything I did or mistrust anyone I spoke to. She was just kind – and sweary – and she made me laugh within minutes. She was funky, sporting tattoos and bright-pink hair, wearing a cute dress with Converse boots; the type of girl I wrote about in my fiction.

I felt happier instantly being in her presence and she just included Wilby without question, which I loved. She gave him toys from her pram and offered him a biscuit. I remember inwardly cringing as I was leaving the park but I got my shit together and asked her if I could take her number so we could meet up again. She said, 'Yes.'

When Josh and I left the park he gave me a huge forehead kiss and said he was proud of me for making friends because at that point, my trust in most people had pretty much disappeared.

I texted her when I got home and we met up a few days later, then again and again. She had two older children of a similar age to Lula and Edie and we would all meet up and do stuff together. It was amazing, but it also made me begin to question stuff with Wilby when I saw Isaac. They were the same age, had been locked down at the same time and I felt like Dani and I parented really similarly – yet they were worlds apart, developmentally. The most noticeable difference was Isaac could talk and Wilby was non-verbal. I reassured myself this was nothing to worry about because I knew boys developed later. But there were other things, like if we were on a pavement near a main road Dani could tell Isaac to wait if he ran ahead and he would. Wilby wouldn't have understood my instruction if I had even tried. He had no idea what I was saying and he had no awareness of danger. He would walk out in front of cars without even knowing they were a hazard.

Isaac also just coped with life. Despite lockdown, Dani could take him anywhere and he would be fine – enjoy it, even – but Wilby just didn't. The more time I spent with them the more I began to question stuff silently. I went back through my camera roll, back to when Edie was the same age as the two boys and I played videos of her running along pavements, listening to my instructions and sitting up and eating independently. I had pictures of her in supermarket trolleys and at soft play and she would hold little conversations with me. I looked at Wilby, who gagged at any food unless it was puréed and had no idea how to use cutlery. I couldn't take him inside anyone's house, as he was petrified, and even pulling up in the car park of a supermarket sent him into a meltdown. I continued to question why other children seemed to be doing so many things he couldn't and wouldn't.

I remember the worst day was when Dani and I drove over an hour to go to a soft-play centre that was new. The reviews were amazing. I was really looking forward to it. We arrived in the car park and Wilby was fine but the second we walked inside he just went into immediate meltdown. He was screaming and crying, throwing himself around everywhere with no awareness he could hurt himself or another child. Nothing I did would calm him down. I remember all the other parents' stares but, more than anything, I remember looking round the place and seeing so many children who were a similar age to Wilby, but were playing, interacting with one another and having fun. I just didn't get it. I didn't get why certain places made him like this. I knew I was going to cry. My cheeks were burning and my neck and chest turned red and blotchy with anxiety. I couldn't swallow, the lump in my throat was growing bigger. I could tell Dani knew too so she just took Wilby off me and whisked him away. I took Isaac and we went and played but I could hear Wilby's screams still from the other end of the huge space. I honestly have never heard a baby cry like Wilby cries. His cries were so penetrating and I didn't know how to make it better. Every child I have raised can be calmed with reassurances, cuddles and, at the very worst, a lollipop, but none of this worked for Wilby. It was almost like he was in another world in which everyone trying to calm and love him was totally invisible to him and it just got worse and worse.

It was around this time that I was massively struggling to balance work and childcare. Jo – who is an old friend and the managing director of my company – and I were filming adverts and trying to sort another book deal whilst I was also in the throes of opening our first women's centre. One day I saw Lucy on the school run. She is the younger sister of my best friend from school, Hayley, and their mum, Debbie, had fostered me for a while when I was fifteen. We began chatting and I told her how I was struggling to get childcare because of the issues I had with Wilby starting nursery and I didn't want to put him through it again. She immediately offered to look after him. She had four daughters, two at Edie's school and two who both had special needs and were autistic. They went to different local special schools. Her youngest used a wheelchair and at times was really poorly. She also had appointments constantly at hospitals, both locally and out of area. Because of this Lucy was unable to work and she also wouldn't be able to have Wilby during the holidays because caring for her daughter was a full-time job, but she was happy to have him between school hours in the week, as and when she could. The relief was immediate because she is the most loving, kind and patient mum and I knew he couldn't be looked after any better.

For the first few weeks she came to my house, so that Wilby got to know her in his own space and he liked her straight away. He was unsettled for the first week at her house – nothing like the start of nursery – but once he learnt his routine and knew he came home at 3 p.m. each day he was fine and then, on a Monday, when we pulled up to her house his whole body would shake and he would flap his hands and squeal with excitement.

I'll never forget the day she said it.

It was 23 September 2021 and Wilby had just turned two.

My builder, Mark, was in the front of the house. Mark used to work for me years ago on renovations when I was a facilities manager for a private care company. He's Mancunian, married to Emma and they have two daughters, and he idolises them all. When I originally met him he instantly reminded me of all the good parts of my dad. Mark was just one of life's decent men and works hard to provide for his family whilst spurring his wife on to do what she loves. He was forever running round after his girls and their friends and, whenever he talks about them, he speaks with such love.

When we bought our house in 2019, he started doing work for us, so he was around most weeks, sometimes every day for weeks or months. The kids almost looked at him as a grandad and Betsy would chat to him all the time about the most random stuff.

I'd just got in from my school run with the kids and Lucy had just finished hers. She walked in behind me as usual with Wilby but, rather than giving me a quick hand-over and running back out the door like she always did, she nervously hung around. I asked her if everything was OK and she asked if she could talk to me. My tummy did a flip though I had no idea why. We sat on the sofa together and she said, 'I don't know how to tell you this, Rach, but have you ever thought that Wilby could be autistic?'

I remember my stomach doing somersaults and the tears just coming before I had even processed what she was saying. I immediately felt so many things. The first thing I felt was guilt and shame that she had two daughters with such significant needs, one of whom will most probably never be able to live independently, and here she was comforting me about my son when we had no idea what was actually going on. I kept apologising for that, for being so selfish and she just kept reassuring me that what I was feeling was fine, even though I didn't actually know what I was feeling. I asked her why she thought he was autistic and when she reeled the list off I realised there was so much I was in denial about. There were so many traits I had ignored or pretended weren't there and I had constantly blamed and hated lockdown for the way Wilby was when, deep down, I only had to look around at other children his age to see that really, none of his behaviours were caused by the pandemic.

She left shortly after and I just didn't know what to do. All the kids were playing with Wilby in the lounge but I couldn't stop crying. I went out to the car to get the shopping out of the boot and was met by Mark, who was cutting wood. The whole scene was caught on our CCTV camera and I downloaded it to my phone. On the bad days I play it back and remember how far we've come.

He gave me a hug when he saw me walk out the door and said, 'Hey, hey, hey, what's up?' in his dad-like, thick Mancunian accent.

I just spat out everything Lucy had said, at first still in denial. 'She thinks he's autistic but he's a lockdown baby,' and, 'I just think he's too tiny for anyone to know he's actually autistic.'

He paused for ages then leant back against his truck and I could tell his mind was spinning with how to say to me what he was thinking. His words will stay with me for ever. 'You know, Rach, I never would have admitted this to you before today, but for the last few weeks I've been going back home to Emma at night and saying, "Something's different with that little lad, he's not doing what he should be doing and he can do extraordinary things he shouldn't be able to do." I asked her if she thought I should speak to you and Josh but she said no, so I didn't, because I was worried I'd upset you. I was worried you wouldn't be ready to hear it or accept it if I told you so I stayed quiet. The fact that girl has had the balls to walk in your house and tell you what she just has makes her very brave, much braver than me.'

I just broke.

He hugged me and reassured me it would be fine and then Josh pulled into the driveway. We went in the house and I told him what both Lucy and Mark had said. I expected him to be as shocked as me, to be angry maybe, confused or in denial. I think, ultimately, I just wanted something from him to make the situation better, to make me feel better — because it was what he had always done, it was what he was good at, but he said nothing. He just looked at the floor of the middle lounge, then the tears came. He just started really crying and said, 'I'm so sorry, darling.' He buried his head onto my shoulder and I knew. I knew right then, without any doubt, that our little boy was autistic, but I had no idea what that actually meant or what it was going to look like but I felt really frightened and totally out of my depth.

Turned out Josh had been secretly researching autism for a few months. By the time I'd had 'the chat' he already knew so much and every question I asked out loud he met with an answer.

It wasn't long before we had Wilby's 2.3-year check. I knew what was coming, as beforehand they send out hefty worksheet/booklet style things for you to complete. Every single question bar a few were things Wilby couldn't do. The health visitor stayed for what seemed like for ever. She then told us that Wilby 'red-flagged' in every single area of her developmental assessment. He was non-verbal, he didn't understand any communication with us, his parents, even 'basic instructions'. He couldn't jump, couldn't hop, he had no danger awareness and he wasn't where he should be with his eating because he had huge sensory issues with certain foods and he couldn't use cutlery. He couldn't unscrew lids on jars, his fine motor skills weren't where they should be, he didn't do any imaginative play or show affection 'like he should'. When he liked certain things in front of the health visitor he showed it by flapping his hands and spinning round in circles until he was dizzy, and his whole body would shudder. He would run past something he had stacked or lined repeatedly and look at it from the corner of his eye and he constantly walked round on his tiptoes.

I repeatedly pointed out to the health visitor his strengths – that he could put his toys or sweets in a line so straight I couldn't do better with a spirit level, that he knew how to stack anything such as blocks or the cushions from the sofa with such precision that they wouldn't tumble or fall even when they were taller than him. If we took him somewhere once that he loved he would remember the exact location for ever and whenever we would go again he would lead the way. This could be the palm tree outside Wagamama in Plymouth. As soon as we parked the car he would lead the five-minute walk to that palm tree from the car park like he had been there a million times; he would do the same walking from our house to the sculptures of cows, a fifteen-minute walk away from home along roads, paths and a park, but he would just know how to get there. We stayed in a caravan in north Devon and he found a 'route' on his first day that he loved, on which he would stop and look at various things. Every day for four days he would just do this route, time and time again, and Josh and I would just follow him round.

'These are not the skills we are looking for,' was all I was met with every time I attempted to point out more of his incredible abilities.

We were immediately referred to paediatrics. And yet, at the time of writing, we've had nothing except a letter saying we are on the waiting list and a booklet for us to fill in at home. That was over a year ago.

I am told the wait for a paediatric appointment should be around a year where I live, sometimes longer. Then the wait for the educational psychologist is around another two years, again maybe longer. You're looking at *years*. Years and years before you get a diagnosis currently. It's a system that's currently broken and it's unfair on both children and their carers and you have to fight to get any kind of support. This isn't OK, but it's better if you know how to fight, if you're in a situation where you can use your voice and you have the energy to fight, but many families don't know how to do this. They are so exhausted trying to cope that the situation spirals downwards very quickly and I just feel it's desperately unfair that there are such ridiculous wait times and lack of services and support when we are talking about a child's health needs and the impact this then puts on a parent's mental health.

The diagnosis

We decided to go private; I know how fortunate we are to have this option now. If Wilby had been born prior to 2017 we never would have been able to afford this, as so many parents can't. I felt really guilty; it almost makes you feel like you're jumping the queue and skipping the heart-ache, but then I spoke to a local educational psychologist who reminded me that people who can go private should. As well as getting their diagnosis quicker it also frees up space in the never-ending NHS queue which means someone else who can't go private gets seen quicker. She actually smiled after she explained it like that and said, 'Look at it like you're doing your bit.'

Wilby was assessed by a team consisting of a psychologist, paediatrician and speech and language and occupational therapists.

For part of the assessment, he was to go with one parent to a centre where two of the team tried to interact with him whilst the entire session was filmed. We decided Josh should go. I was still really emotional with it all at that point and when Wilby melts down Josh just copes much better, plus he's physically stronger and better able to manage him when he has a really bad physical outburst.

During the hour-long assessment, Josh told me that Wilby was 'just Wilby'. He was really emotional upon entering the room with strangers. Once he calmed he became obsessed over certain toys to the point he flapped, side-eyed and shuddered on his tiptoes. He refused to make any eye contact with the team but still caught the ball they threw him from the other side of the room from different angles and distances. He had a meltdown when the team took those toys away. Other toys he refused to engage with because they were of no interest to him, such as those involving imaginative play and feeding a baby doll her dinner. He lined his sweets in a perfect line, he became fixated on opening and closing the door and when

Josh tried to transition him to do something else he physically attacked him.

All in all in that sixty minutes Josh was confident they'd seen every part of Wilby they needed to see.

The team emailed us to tell us they would need to have one more meeting the following Friday and they would then meet as a team with all their findings, watch the video of his assessment and make their decision on his diagnosis or decide whether they'd work with him further to explore things in more detail before they could finalise their report.

It got to 10 a.m. the following Friday and the psychologist opened by saying, 'Before we go any further I don't feel there is any point in keeping you waiting any more as the whole team has made a decision. I know it won't come as any shock to you that we have given Wilby an autism diagnosis.'

It did, though.

I remember feeling like I had been punched in the stomach. I began to cry. I had no idea why I was crying.

I knew I wanted this diagnosis. I needed it. I'd already envisaged them coming back to me and saying he wasn't autistic and that feeling filled me with sheer panic. I'd imagined it happening and me saying, 'Well, what the fuck do I do now?' because I had no clue how to manage him . . . but still, we were here, he had his diagnosis and I felt so unbelievably sad and guilty. I felt guilty for feeling sad when he was so perfect.

What I loved about the rest of that meeting and his assessment report when it hit my inbox was how the team concentrated on his strengths. They pointed out all of his good points, the stuff he could do that was just incredible. All the stuff I had pointed out at his most recent check that had been ignored or I'd been repeatedly told it was 'not what they're looking at'.

I realised then that those NHS forms, developmental checks and assessments are made for neurotypical children. They're not made for neurodiverse children and it made me really sad, because there are so many neurodiverse children in the world. Yet when that comes to light for us as parents for the first time it's seen as a 'red flag', as a 'concern'. There are no reassurances when it happens. You're not left with any leaflets on all the positive bits of having a child with ASD (autism spectrum disorder). After that developmental check I was left with the same feeling I had when I got the, 'We can't see a heartbeat – we need to send you for another scan,' when I lost three babies.

It's panic, it's fear, it's the unknown. The 'fucking hell, how is this happening to me' feeling. There was not one single positive feeling I had when that health visitor left that day, yet I had just showed her the most incredible little boy with so many strengths and skills.

That is why I then made the decision to show Wilby off, because it's so important people see the signs of a child that's autistic. I feel so ashamed looking back that, when I had been in denial, I posted him on social media when he looked like every other child his age. I cut the parts out where he flapped and went on his tiptoes, I constantly covered my Instagram Stories with music so people wouldn't notice his noises and I repeatedly ignored the 'Is he talking yet?' messages that hit my inbox. I realised after the chat I had with Lucy, that first developmental check and on getting his diagnosis that it's so important for people to see how he flaps and side-eyes and walks on tiptoes for a whole half an hour when he fixates on a palm tree, but it's also just as important for me that they see the meltdowns when he has to transition away from that palm tree.

Some days, no amount of countdowns, PECS cards (visual aids that show ASD children, as simply as possible, what activities they are undertaking now and what they will be doing next), sand timers or verbal prompts are going to stop Wilby attacking Josh or me. We may have chunks of hair missing or he may draw blood. He self-harms because he has no idea how to regulate himself, so he will smash his head off any surface he can find or he gouges at his own skin until it bleeds. He can hit and kick and spit and pull and push and more in public because he has lost all control. Neither Josh nor I, as adults, as his parents – and Josh is over six foot tall and a physically fit man – can manage those situations.

Wilby is so incredibly strong when he goes into emotional crisis that neither of us stand a chance until he calms down, and for me it's so important that people see this. People should start having an awareness that this isn't a naughty child with a mum who can't manage. This isn't a situation you should judge or ignore. It's a situation you should absolutely approach and ask, 'Tell me what I can do to help you.' At the very worst the parent is going to say, 'Nothing, leave us alone,' and what then? You walk away, but you walk away knowing you tried.

If someone approached me and asked if they could help, I would accept, even if it was just to have someone to grab his bag or pram so I can stop Wilby hurting himself, even if it was someone I could cry to whilst they sat next to me on the pavement, even if it was someone just to stand alongside me and say nothing so I didn't feel so alone. Most of the time being a mum of a little boy who's autistic is the best job in the world, but some days, just some occasional days, it's the hardest and on those days it honestly takes a village; without that it's one of the loneliest, most isolating places I have ever been.

It's a journey

What I will say to anyone on this journey is that it's OK to cry. I remember when I went on my Instagram Stories after Wilby's 2.3-year check (I saved this to highlights in case you want to watch it, under 'Wilby 1').

I mentioned he might be autistic and I was crying. I got backlash from people asking me why I was crying when 'autism is a gift', telling me how disrespectful I was being to autistic people and I felt sick. On the other hand, I also get so many people telling me how I should talk about Wilby.

What offends some people is absolutely OK with others and vice versa, so I do my best to educate myself with the least offensive terminology and the most respectful language and I talk. On the days I get shit in my inbox or I feel doubts I remind myself that this is my journey, that the Instagram page is my life and this has been hard. So fucking hard. And I'm doing my best, the only way I know how.

At the start Josh and I cried daily. Every single day. Some days him more than me. I remember someone recommended we watch *The A Word* on the BBC, a drama about a family's journey to their little boy getting an autism diagnosis, with all the bits before and after, and we sat and binged all three series, and every night we paused the TV to cry together – always at the same parts. It was like therapy for us.

I remember one mum saying to me she felt like she was grieving after she got her daughter's diagnosis, for the life she had planned for her, for all the toddler groups and swimming clubs she had envisaged in her head. She had grieved for what she thought she was getting and I just totally understood it.

If a professional could stand in front of me and tell me Wilby's future I would have been OK. If I got a, 'He will never cope with mainstream education and he will always be non-verbal,' I would have known, I could have planned for that future. If they'd said, 'He will be in the mainstream with support and he will be talking within a year,' I'd have coped. But I couldn't get that, I can't ever get that – because that's the thing: no one knows what his future looks like.

I wouldn't change Wilby for the world. If I had the option to go back and birth him again and for him not to be autistic I wouldn't do it, because I have never seen a child as happy as Wilby. That bubble he lives in is magical. To watch a child get such joy from things like a car driving past at speed, a palm tree blowing in the wind or making lines and lines of animal toys is phenomenal, but I still don't know what his future looks like. And I'm frightened, not for me, but for him. I constantly worry about people staring at him when he is a teenager, flapping on his tiptoes in the park. I'm worried that if we get one of his school settings wrong other kids will see he's 'different' to them and people will be unkind. I am absolutely fucking terrified for his future but that's not because of him, it's because of other people in this world. It's because I already know for Wilby to thrive people need to climb into his bubble, they need to live in his world rather than trying to make him conform to theirs and I worry about how many people in life will do that for him.

But it does get easier.

I came across a page on Instagram of a lady who special-ises in supporting children with ASD. I looked through her posts and highlights and one night I reached out to her and broke my heart in her inbox. She was just incredible, to the point that we now speak most days – she always cheers on Wilby's good days and little wins, and she breaks things down to me about why he might do the things he does on his bad days. When something feels particularly hard and I don't know how to manage a certain behaviour or situation I will send her a video or a voice note and she explains in simple terms why Wilby will be acting like he is, the feelings he gets from certain things he does. She supports me in trying to either help him to move on or support him to cope. Recently she recommended getting him a backpack with something weighted in it that he likes, so I filled it with his animal toys and popped it on his back. He absolutely loves it and now picks it up to wear it every time we leave the house. The weight in the bag helps him regulate and when I shared it on my page so many people messaged. Teachers said that they get their teenage ASD students to move heavy tables around when they're anxious and it calms them, mums said how their sons are given 'jobs' from teachers to move piles of books to the library or reams of A4 paper to the photocopier. More importantly I get messages from other mums trying to navigate their way along this journey who had no idea weighted bags or blankets were a thing, as I didn't – and they are forever grateful I shared it because in turn it's helped them and their children. That is the joy of social media, the positive impact it has. Finding that incredible lady has been a lifeline on so many occasions and it reminds me of all the good things social media brings.

We also managed to get some portage support – the home-visiting educational service for preschool children with special needs. A lady came to the house to play with Wilby for an hour a week and recommended a preschool for us that she thought would suit him. I felt so anxious and my immediate reaction was to decline because of the experience with the first nursery, but also because I wasn't sure if I was ready to share him with strangers just yet. Still, Josh said we should go and view it, because he thought it could be a positive thing. As soon as we arrived, I felt emotional. Wilby strolled in like he knew the way and his excitement at his surroundings – the toys, watching the other children interact, the activities – all of it was really beautiful to see. He just went off and played. He didn't look at us, or for us, and the teachers and assistants formed one of the nicest groups of women I've ever encountered. They were genuinely lovely – not just to the children but to each other and they were fun. It was the type of preschool that felt like home, like I would want to do the school run there. I wouldn't get that sick, worried feeling waiting for him to come out because they made it feel so welcoming and lovely. And so he started recently. He is doing three days a week and to date he loves it.

It's part mainstream and part SEN (special education needs). They have already called a meeting to look at his learning development plan, as they are struggling with some of the things Wilby fixates on. I felt a bit worried when they asked us to meet with the SEN teacher but then I had to remind myself it's a good thing that they are trying to work out the best ways to help Wilby cope so he is able to do all kinds of incredible things. It's lovely that they include us in that – to ask what our thoughts and feelings are so that we can all be structured and doing the same thing for Wilby, who thrives on routine.

They have just put together a report to undertake his EHCP, a care plan to ensure he gets the support he needs during his education. Again, it made a pretty sad read – but they have to focus on the bad days and all the stuff he can't do, that makes him vulnerable – to ensure he gets the best shot at an education and more importantly, being happy and included in his school setting. He is due to go to panel next month where people I don't know will make a decision on what type of education my son gets. It's daunting, it's scary but I truly believe he will be OK. Josh and I are able to advocate for him and he has five elder siblings who I know will always take care of him.

It's been almost a year since Lucy sat down with me and asked to 'have a word'. I still cry, Josh still cries, but not as often. Last week we went to the fair and he had his worst meltdown to date, after not having had one for eleven days. We both left the fair battered, bruised and embarrassed at the stares. We got home and had a little cry, but we also celebrated that he had managed eleven days without that. Almost two weeks of him coping day and night with so many transitions and changes which is incredible. We always remember the positives when we discuss the negatives, because they far outweigh them, even on the bad days.

I've cried writing this chapter; I've had to shut the laptop several times and come back. Josh has read it and had a cry, remembering the last twelve months, seeing how far we've come and how we felt back then, compared to now. It feels really emotional for us but, honestly, I'd go through it all again, a thousand times, to have had the highs we get parenting Wilby, because he is just the most incredible little boy in the world and I know he has taught Josh, me and his brothers and sisters so much already. Him being around has made us better people with a load more understanding about the world we live in and I hope that in sharing our journey we raise some awareness which helps others.

4

GROWING UP

Just after Lucy and I had 'the chat' and Wilby's journey became a reality for us, Tallulah was due to return to school after lockdown.

It was September 2021 and she was going into year eight.

Tallulah has always found school a struggle, from when she first started reception aged four and a half. I first moved her primary schools in 2006, when she was six years old, because I felt she just didn't fit in. She wasn't part of any friendship group in her year and, although she would mention random names from her class, she never got invited to anyone's house for dinner, she never wanted to invite anyone and on the days I saw the kids in her class hand out party invites she rarely got one. It made me feel sad, because Betsy, Seb and Isaac were thriving, making friends, getting invited for dinner at their friends' houses and to parties at soft play and constantly having friends over to ours.

. When she moved school she made a best friend who the teachers asked her to buddy with. They were inseparable straight away. Her friend was really quiet and idolised Lula and Lula was able to be 'Lula' around her without ever being judged. It was the Lula we saw at home, the Lula who said what she wanted without thinking and even if she did think, she still said what she wanted. She was loud – often too loud – but she had a smile so wide it landed her with two huge dimples that lit up a room.

Lula never liked 'normal stuff' that kids her age liked. Instead, she preferred to hang out with her flock of chickens in the back garden and she would spend hours pottering around B&Q then make beautiful hanging baskets. She would spend hours researching the best way to make slime, then use her birthday money to purchase products like washing detergent from the USA and tiny, coloured foam beads and spend for ever on the perfect slime recipe that she would play with day and night. Her first best friend did all this with Lula and they just loved being together for the next four years.

When they went into their last year at primary a shift happened. Other girls had formed friendship groups and Lula and her friend couldn't work out whether they did or didn't want to be involved. It caused such issues. Both girls would break their heart over the bitchiness that often comes with being in a group of girls and their friendship was really broken at times. Lula would stay in with the teachers at lunch and, when it came to choosing their secondary schools, her best friend went to the local one with all the other girls and Lula was adamant she wanted to go to a different one out of town where she knew no one. Josh tried so hard to talk her out of it but she was having none of it. Her best friend begged her to go to the same school but there was no changing her mind, so she left primary and started a new secondary in a different town with a whole bunch of new kids.

Lula has always been really close to my mum (who moved near us when the girls were little) and none of the others have ever been the way Lula is with her. My mum made Lula her own bedroom at her house and she would stay there every Wednesday. They would spend most weekends together, going to garden centres, making incredible artwork and baking all kinds of cakes and crumbles. It reminded me of the times I had visited my mum in Louth, Lincolnshire, when I was a little girl. After she left, when I was four, I only saw her a few times a year, when she was so hands on with me, and we were busy doing all sorts of amazing things together. It always left me really confused as to why I wasn't living with her full-time, or at all.

When Lula wasn't at Mum's or at school, she was mainly with me. Betsy stopped seeing their dad as much in 2016 and the final time she saw him was 2017. There was an incident in which Tallulah got a splinter in her foot – she freaked over her dad getting the splinter out and went into a meltdown. He lost his temper with Tallulah and Betsy lost hers with him. I think everything Betsy had kept inside for the past thirteen years came out that night and he couldn't cope that he was being spoken to like that. I suppose the realisation hit that he had finally lost all control over her.

She called me, crying, from the bathroom and I drove over to his girlfriend's house to collect her. He refused to let Lula leave but Betsy reassured me that she was fine and was playing with his girlfriend's children and her parents were now there. He came towards my car and lost it with both of us verbally. Betsy screamed back, 'I promise you will never see me again!'

I swallowed a lump of every emotion possible, just put my foot down and drove to the next street. I pulled the car up and cradled my eldest baby and we sat for a good ten minutes and sobbed together. We didn't say anything. I held her face next to mine and we had a full-blown crying fit. There was so much we needed to talk about, so many things we were feeling, so many apologies I needed to make, explanations I needed to give, but right there wasn't the time, so we gained some composure, wiped our tears, blew our noses and drove home with her hand gripping mine. She has, however, kept her promise, and she's never seen him since.

This meant that Lula began seeing her dad alone every other weekend. Her anxiety was off the scale and in hindsight I'm not sure where my head was at, but that's the thing – you do it because you feel you have no other option. You do it because you don't know you can't. It's a decision that often keeps me awake at night to this day.

Lula was under paediatrics at Torbay hospital during these years because she used to get so unwell. She would constantly get water infections and pass blood in her urine. She would be up all night at least once a week and miss school regularly because she was so tired. Whenever it happened whilst she was in her dad's care he would get so angry he would drop her home, sometimes in the middle of the night. Josh and I would hear the door banging and she would be stood there in her dressing gown in tears and her dad would be so frustrated. He would rant at me on my doorstep in the early hours about it being a 'fucking joke', that I need to 'get her sorted' and 'get to the bottom of it'. She would walk in the house and up to the sofa and I would pacify him, promising I would sort it before he stormed off, like he was so hard done by, without saying goodbye to his youngest daughter. I hate the control he had even then, looking back now.

She had kidney scans, blood tests, everything. In the end the paediatrician asked me if there was anything going on emotionally at home that could be causing it because, physically, they could find nothing wrong.

The weekend of my book being published in 2018 was the last time Lula ever saw her dad. That book coming out sent him over the edge and the person on the receiving end of his frustrations and irritation was his nine-year-old daughter in the car on her way to school on the Monday morning.

The build-up to Lula's return to school in year eight was horrendous. Her year seven had been a write-off because of Covid and she hadn't made any proper friends. I was away working out of the area for a week and, whilst I was gone, there were some incidents at school which were really bad. Some girls went for Lula, and sent her voice notes on WhatsApp that they deleted but not before Betsy had heard them. They were horrific. They bullied her over social media and in the school canteen. She was in such a state she had a huge meltdown at home. Betsy didn't want to worry me on the tour so she booked a meeting with Lula at her school the following day and bossed it. She took Lula home with her after the meeting, refusing to let her stay because she wanted to give the school time to sort the issues and implement changes but nothing really improved. Lula spent her days eating her lunch alone and avoiding certain people who repeatedly took the piss out of her skin and said her hair was greasy. She quickly began to hate herself and, by this point, I was really frightened.

At the beginning of September she came home from school and had the worst meltdown I've ever seen, due to another incident. I immediately called her school and had a lengthy chat with her pastoral teacher who was really lovely and supportive. As Lucy had done with Wilby, she had the difficult conversation with me – she wanted to get an urgent referral to an educational psychologist because she believed Lula also had ASD. This time it was almost a relief to hear it. Betsy and Seb had always said, since she was about seven, that they thought she was autistic. I cried down the phone.

The teacher said, 'I am never one for children moving schools because I believe in fixing the problem but if a child isn't happy, they aren't learning and Lula has never been happy at this school.'

And so, I didn't send her back. Instead I sat and researched ASD in teenage girls and was again left flooded with guilt. For so many years Lula had worked really hard to mask her autism and fit in with her surroundings and she had just gone under the radar. Until it happens to you, you have no awareness and I was so upset. I hated that this must be happening daily to many, many kids, yet I had never educated my own kids how to help or support them because I didn't even know it was a thing until I had to do research for our family. It really sucked.

Betsy came home and I told her what the school had said about Lula getting assessed and she just said matter of factly, 'But we all know she's autistic, Mum. We've known for years. We've said it for years.' And we had, kind of. But deep down I suppose I convinced myself she was a little eccentric, different to the others in a weird and wonderful way and I thought as she grew she would just be more like them. The reality was that masking autism in girls is a real thing and it gets harder as they get older and it was clear to us all that now she was simply exhausted. She was absolutely tired of pretending to be someone she wasn't and becoming a teenager made it so much harder to slot in.

I called her into the garden and told her that her pastoral teacher had mentioned her being autistic. I asked her what she thought and she said once again, like she'd said many times over many years, 'I'm just different, Mum. I'm so different to everyone.' This time she continued trying to explain her feelings through her tears. She told me people didn't see her. I asked what she meant and she said, 'They just don't see me, not the real me.' She kept repeating this but couldn't explain what she meant.

By this point Lula was hyperventilating with tears and couldn't regulate her emotions at all. My heart broke for her. We both sobbed that day together in the garden. Lula is the least affectionate child of all of ours, but she just put her whole body into mine. We cried together at what was to come because we knew we had absolutely no idea and felt massively out of our depth.

The following week we viewed the secondary school her best friend had started a year earlier. We met with the

SENCO (special educational needs coordinator), pastoral lead and head of year and they spent two hours talking mostly to Lula, not me, which felt refreshing. They asked her everything and I watched her answer these questions. She giggled, but she also cried because, like she had been telling me for years, she 'felt different' and I was so proud of her for being brave enough to tell three adult strangers she had only just met about what went on inside her brain.

She said she wasn't the same as the girls within her school. She didn't have the same likes or interests and when she pretended she did so that she 'fitted in', she became exhausted. She explained what caused her anxiety. Things I didn't know, such as teachers changing the seating plans without any warning, the school reviewing sets so there was a chance she would move classes and be around new people and even having to take her socks off in PE.

Lula has heavy periods and is on a three-week cycle so she needs to have permission to go to the toilet when she needs to go. The build-up to having to ask or being told to wait until breaktime causes her anxiety. She said she hated having to answer questions out loud in class; the panic she felt at a teacher choosing her to publicly talk in front of the class terrified her. She also explained how often she would go off into a trance and would miss up to half the lesson day-dreaming and then she would get into trouble with the teacher because she couldn't complete the work.

They would accuse her of not listening. She explained that she couldn't physically stop her body going off into a trance and it upset her that she didn't have this control no matter how hard she tried. The meeting made me really emotional, to think that I honestly had no idea how tough school had been for her.

The SENCO was amazing and reassured Tallulah that everything she was feeling could be solved easily by putting notes on the system so that teachers were aware. She would also get a pass so she could leave class at any time without question if she needed the toilet or felt overwhelmed. She reassured her that her seating space would remain the same or that she would not be moved without prior meeting with her support staff. The SENCO recommended ploughing ahead with the referral for a diagnosis and was really honest with us both; she told Lula that she felt she was autistic with some sensory processing issues.

I explained to the school the relationship Lula and her best friend had had for years and the way the SENCO explained it made total sense. Sometimes, when someone is autistic, they make one key friend. It works well because the autistic person is either the 'leader' and the person who isn't autistic follows everything the autistic person does quite happily or vice versa. However, if someone else gets involved in the friendship group, it breaks down or becomes distant for some reason, then very often the autistic person doesn't cope. They've put everything they have into it and they don't know what to do. They have become totally reliant upon that other person to exist and survive.

This seemed to be what had happened with Tallulah before she left primary school and I honestly don't think she was now coping without her best friend. Lula is a hundred per cent the leader and I constantly thank her best friend for being so patient and understanding because at times she is not an easy friend to have. Lula changed schools and we have had issues because it's now no longer just her and her best friend. They spent over a year apart during which time the friend had to make new relationships. Lula has had to fit into a whole new group, which has been really hard at times. Only this week she has had two days off school because they've all fallen out – which is normal, and expected – but Lula acts totally differently to everyone else within the group. She is black-and-white, she isn't emotional until she goes into a meltdown, which can be really upsetting and sometimes frightening to watch. She says everything she thinks and feels without any thought of how she might come across. The school have worked really hard this week on doing restorative work with the whole friendship group, but mostly they have worked to educate everyone about Lula, on why she thinks and feels the way she does, on why, just because she doesn't show emotion like they do or get upset over the same things, doesn't mean she doesn't care or like them.

Her brain works differently to those of most of the girls she hangs out with, and that's OK. They all need to have an understanding of why and how she operates, which I'm really hopeful now that they do.

The issue, as with Wilby, is that we are on a two-to-three-year wait for diagnosis. Tallulah will be sixteen before we're there, a brutal age anyway let alone one to get a diagnosis of autism.

She has the most incredible pastoral teacher who she meets with weekly now and her school have a phenomenal ASD suite with a therapy dog that she can dip into if she needs to.

The meltdowns are still very much present and she is marked as having ASD within the school so teachers give her the understanding she needs. Sometimes we will go weeks of having nothing but positive days but then something will happen. It would be something really silly to me or the other big kids, but to Lula it feels huge, and I have to remind myself, and her siblings, that her brain works differently to ours. When something seems petty to us we have to have the understanding that it's totally overwhelming for Lula.

On these days it's really tough; she presents totally differently. She can be through the roof with excitement and really loud to the point she shouts instead of talks. She doesn't take a breath and she isn't actually speaking for you to listen. She's just helping herself regulate. Other days she melts down. She will go to the toilets in school and refuse to come out. Either she or her best friend will call me and she can send me or Betsy over a hundred text messages in the space of a minute, ordering us to go to school and collect her, getting angry if we don't reply immediately. It's full on and it's exhausting. Luckily, her school are incredible. Her pastoral worker just deals with it. She calls me and simply says, 'Sorted,' before talking me through everything she's done to bring Lula back down to earth.

I feel like now Lula has the awareness of ASD her masking has almost stopped. It's still there around certain people or in new or uncertain situations but overall she's a totally different Lula to the one she's been for years. This is hard some days, because everything in Lula's world continues to be black-and-white. She struggles to show any emotion unless she feels her world is falling apart and I genuinely don't think she feels any empathy towards others. The way she thinks and deals with situations shows that she doesn't think of other people's feelings at all at times.

Only on one occasion have I seen her breaking her heart for someone else, which was her big sister, and I think that was because she could see no one had any control over that situation. Betsy lost all control during lockdown and had an incident where she was physically violent and it petrified Tallulah so she just needed us to make it better in whatever way possible. Lula is honest, which isn't a bad thing – until she thinks Betsy's nose looks big or doesn't like Edie's hair style, or she doesn't like the dinner Josh has made. When I explain to her the way in which she says things could hurt someone's feelings she genuinely looks at me like I have two heads. In Lula's world she is telling the truth. In her world Betsy's nose did look big in the picture she just took, Edie's hair looked better before she had it cut and she hated the sauce Josh used with spaghetti, so why shouldn't she just be honest about those things? And I get her logic, because ultimately she's not being unkind or trying to hurt people. She just doesn't have that awareness and I'm unsure if she ever will know that she hurts people's feelings.

A prime example recently was when she went camping in her friend's garden and Betsy lent her a tent. She explained to Lula how to erect it properly. Lula arrived at the sleepover and her friend's dad started to sort the tents. Lula wanted to do her own tent the way Betsy had told her, because it was Betsy's tent and she had promised to look after it as Betsy had said. Her friend's dad started telling Lula his way was the best way and Lula just wouldn't have it to the point she was called rude. She was really upset because in her head she wasn't being rude and I know she was being Lula. I asked her best friend if she 'appeared' rude and she looked at Lula and giggled and said, 'Yeah, she seemed rude'. Lula got really upset because she couldn't cope with the concept that people thought badly of her.

The following week the same girl's dad gave Lula a lift to school. I asked how it went as she thought he didn't like her and she said, 'Yeah, fine. On the way to school I said, "Just so you know: I'm not rude, I think I'm autistic".' I was so proud of her for doing that.

It was her way of teaching us to understand her world. People should have more awareness of the fact there are millions of neurodiverse people that live in our world. Most days I look at Wilby and Lula and I would love to live in their worlds and think like they do. I've come to realise it is absolutely our responsibility as neurotypical people to educate ourselves to accept people with ASD and to ensure that, actually, we fit into their worlds, rather than the other way around.

The crossroads

I've focused on Lula having a rough ride with school but actually, all my kids have had encounters whilst they've been at school which have broken their hearts, and mine. Each has struggled at different points as kids do.

Betsy, right now, has just left college. She did social sciences for two years and hated it. She hated the class-room environment. For the first year she attended regularly and completed the work, probably because she had just come out of twelve years of education and still felt like a child but, by the second year, she was transitioning into an adult. Most of her friends were eighteen (she's an August baby, so was still seventeen), she passed her driving test during this time and wanted to earn money to do fun things so started working loads of hours at three different jobs. Her college life began going downhill and this is where I look back and massively regret the way I parented. Her tutor called me one day to say she wasn't happy with pretty much everything – Betsy's attendance, attitude and the work she was producing.

This immediately wound Betsy up because she was being managed differently to all her friends who were doing the same stuff. But they were treated as adults and any issues the college managed directly with them and didn't contact their parents. Just because she was born later in the year she had to answer to her college, and then me. Her tutor asked me to speak to her which I did, but what I didn't do is look at the bigger picture.

I took everything that the tutor had said to me and spat it out at Betsy without thought. I saw what I was told – that she had less than a year left of college and she should change her attitude, work ethic and get it sorted to pass her exams. I didn't see that actually she hated this course, it was making her so unhappy and she was smashing life in all three jobs where she was punctual, hardworking and happy. We ended up having a huge row. To date, we have had three massive rows in her life, neither of us backing down and her storming out. I remind myself constantly that having just three bad rows in eighteen years: it could be worse.

If I could replay 'that day' again I would have taken some time to process the call with her tutor, then I would have chatted to Betsy and sympathised with her that it sucked that I get calls and none of her mates' parents do. I would have listened to her and remembered that eight months felt like such a short space of time to me and her teachers, but she was having to turn up to a college course every day which she dreaded, to the point she had that awful feeling in the pit of her belly. In hindsight I would have praised her for working her arse off in three jobs for minimum wage, but hindsight is a beautiful (infuriating) thing and instead I told her she needed to knuckle down and sort her life out and get the results she was originally predicted and had been getting twelve months earlier. I told her I didn't care that her friends' parents weren't being called, I was going to manage her like the college asked me to. When she was at the point of losing control of her anger because she could see I wasn't listening to her, I told her she reminded me of her dad.

Urgh. I've just felt a little belly flip and a hot flush writing this down because I am so upset and ashamed that I would ever say that to her. As soon as the words left my mouth and I saw her reaction I felt like vomiting, but I was still raging. Raging at her, raging at her college for implementing weird rules for kids in the same class, raging at myself. I was absolutely fucking devastated at my own actions, that I had told my first-born baby she was like the man we had fled from. The man she had watched perpetrate abuse for the first six and a half years of her life, and who, when I left, had made her the main target for the next seven years until she made the decision that she didn't want to see him again.

She stormed out that day, like she had twice before, only this time she left with packed bags and told Seb on her way out she wouldn't be coming back.

That feeling I get when something isn't right between me and my babies is the worst. I hate going to bed angry and upset, I hate fighting and falling out with them when things are left unresolved but I'm also massively stubborn. I'll go into more detail about this later but I remember my dad saying how much I sulked when I was little, and I did. I remember my mum living in Birmingham and, when I went up to stay with her, all her friends in the pub would call me a mardy arse, and I was. And at times I still am, I've really worked on it in the last few years through therapy and understanding why I behave this way. The only one it affects really is me, and it's a pretty shit feeling to stay angry or upset. Who wants to live life like that?

Betsy came back after ten days. I began checking in with her college daily but to be honest, the things her tutor was saying to me about how she thought Betsy was feeling and the reasons why wound me up and made me really emotional so I went through to the pastoral lead who was incredible and did a lot of work with Betsy which massively helped us both. When Betsy came home we sat in the kitchen and talked for hours, then she spoke with Josh, then the three of us spoke together.

Betsy has always appeared to have her life together, both to us as her parents and I imagine to you watching her online. She's ridiculously beautiful, she is confident and strong-willed. She's fiercely loyal to her family and friends and she will call out anyone or anything she knows isn't OK, even if she has to go at it alone. She is hardworking and has a huge heart (especially when she spots an elderly person struggling to carry their bags of shopping!) and she's also a gobshite who can be extremely opinionated and rarely backs down, even when she's in the wrong. What that talk also taught me that night is she's actually pretty fucking broken.

She asked me why in the past Seb, Isaac and Lula had all had counselling for what they'd endured through their lives, why they had all spoken to someone and she hadn't. I suppose it was because I blamed all of Lula's behaviours on anxiety so I got her private play therapy. Seb and Isaac were recommended counselling by a charity that supported Josh with the boys in 2017 when they last had contact with their mum.

Betsy had always appeared fine to me, and unaffected. She was strong and funny and I suppose she just took the piss out of her trauma, out of the things we went through together with her dad, but deep down it had totally ruined her and made her question everything and everyone around her. It was another prime example of how, just because someone appears to be more than OK, they can be hiding so much.

After Tallulah stopped seeing her dad in 2018 it went bad for a while. He turned up to our new house and lost his temper on our doorstep.

It then went too quiet – he had never been quiet in the eight years since I had left him. A court summons landed on my mat whilst I was heavily pregnant with Wilby, stating he wanted contact with the girls. The first hearing was in Plymouth family court, when Wilby was a few weeks old and I was still recovering from the caesarean section. I was breastfeeding and feeling really low and vulnerable with the online trolling plus overwhelmed by having just had a baby.

He arrived with a solicitor who was pretty cut-throat. I self-represented. His solicitor spoke for him, while I had to do my own talking every time a question was asked in the courtroom, all while his eyes were burning into me. I wanted to be sick.

A section 7 report was ordered in the first hearing – which is what happens when parents cannot agree and the court needs more information and a CAFCASS (Children and Family Court Advisory and Support Service) officer was appointed to the case to work with both girls to ascertain their wishes and feelings. Their dad was advised to acknowledge how the girls felt and to write them letters of apology.

His letters were passed on to the girls in their first meeting with the CAFCASS worker. Betsy was annoyed to see hers was short whereas Tallulah's was heartfelt, much longer and detailed. Immediately Betsy felt this was about him and his family wanting to see Tallulah, not her. The CAFCASS officer was really good; she understood how Betsy felt. She hadn't seen or spoken to him for years by this point and he had never attempted to make contact with her, yet now he was paying what could be thousands to be represented by one of the best solicitors and it appeared clear this was all about Tallulah. She relayed Betsy's feelings to her dad.

Covid then hit. This meant things were delayed and the girls saw the CAFCASS officer over Zoom, which I feel didn't work as well as it would have in person. The court ordered all the police and children's services logs. The emailed copies hit my inbox from his solicitor on a Friday evening and I don't think I slept that entire weekend. I felt so many things reading through everything. They call it a 'trial bundle'. It's basically all the paperwork from every relevant agency and organisation which is used as evidence, wrapped up in one huge document to help strangers who sit behind a wooden bench make decisions and orders on the futures of my babies. The police logs knocked me sick: I saw the number of times they'd been called out to us by neighbours, and read notes by professionals who the children at my house had disclosed things to.

One of the police logs records a time they came to Betsy's school playground when I was dropping her off to speak to me. I remember that day so well. I imagine the police felt it would be less inflammatory to see me there rather than coming to our house, where Betsy's dad still was at that time, but I couldn't have felt more terrified with the number of eyes watching me. I believed someone would feed back to him that they were there trying to talk and I begged them to leave me alone. That particular police log was made because the neighbours had called them when they heard an incident in our house, and saw him come out minutes later, raging.

I'll tell you what got me about one of the police log sheets (I still have them all to hand now): officers wrote two separate entries on the same sheet, a week apart – the first reads, 'Female does not want any positive action taken. Not engaging with police. Recently suffered miscarriage. Relationship stressful, children in the house all the time.' The second, four days later reads, 'Rachaele is still reluctant to make a statement. She does not want him arrested or spoken to as this would make matters worse.

She is fully aware of force policy and was given DV [domestic violence] advice.'

As I read those logs and write this book it's like I'm looking back at someone else's life. I don't recognise that person as me, despite still remembering all the feelings I had back then of sheer desperation and fear. I genuinely believed my life was in danger if I didn't do exactly what was expected of me and I desperately tried to convince those police officers and everyone around me that what was happening was all my fault. Intervention would put my children and me in even more danger. I blamed that incident – and so many others – on me losing a baby, on us having children around making him feel stressed. I begged them not to arrest him or it would make things worse, and what destroys me the most is that it felt back then, and now, that I was believed.

People must have believed those things I said to leave me there, to not try harder to get me to leave, for the police not to investigate a victimless prosecution. What wrecks my brain is that I know I needed the absolute opposite.

I needed people to reassure me that losing a baby doesn't make someone scream and shout and hurt you in front of your three-year-old child; I needed to know raising children shouldn't stress you out so much it makes you abusive. If they had trawled his mobile phone to see the text threats he sent me, voicemails so loud his voice would crack, or if they spoke to my neighbours properly, they could have easily understood my situation. It would have meant I could have left a whole lot earlier. I could have found the strength in 2007 to pack my and my three-year-old daughter's belongings and flee, but I didn't.

I stayed another three years, had another baby and made up a shitload more excuses to more police officers and neighbours, until I couldn't take it anymore. And the only bonus to come out of that is Tallulah, nothing else.

Fast-forward ten years to us sitting next to each other in a family court and, despite the officials having access to this trial bundle, despite them reading everything that I've mentioned above and more, they still fired questions to the effect that if the father of my children was 'that bad' why did I allow him to continue seeing them after I left? Then there were the comments magistrates made, and I hear it repeatedly: that just because he abuses Mum doesn't mean he cannot be a good father.

GOOD FATHERS DO NOT ABUSE THE MOTHER OF THEIR CHILDREN.

And that question, that question they asked me about me allowing contact after I left? That question they ask to so many thousands of women just like me? A survivor of domestic abuse has been trained to believe by their perpetrator throughout the relationship that they will have their children removed if they don't toe the line.

There is no support or advice readily available for women like us, giving us assurances we can just stop our children seeing that perpetrator. Most domestic abuse survivors leave their relationships and they don't even know what to cook for tea, or what they like to eat because they have been controlled for so long. Yet all of a sudden we are expecting them to navigate their way through family court, against a perpetrator who has destroyed their lives and those of their babies – it's absolutely terrifying. Instead, both parents are given parental responsibility – either one can collect their child from school and withhold them from the other parent. There is nothing there and then to explain to you what you need to do to get support or help. Instead, it's unclear, confusing and daunting.

Family court is a long-winded, drawn out and outdated process where things go wrong. Situations are just not recognised for what they are. It's unjust, unfair, ridiculously costly and fucking frustrating.

After we got the police logs it was back for another court hearing. His solicitor pushed for a final hearing where he would have a barrister to cross-examine me and I would either pay £3,600 for a barrister to cross-examine him or I would have to do it myself. Me, cross-examine a man who had abused me and my children for a decade? I begged the CAFCASS officer and magistrates for it not to go to a final hearing. By this point the CAFCASS officer had worked with the girls, she had listened to four voicemails he had left for Betsy which felt abusive and upsetting. He was refusing to take any responsibility, a lot of the time blaming Betsy for 'winding him up', despite the fact she was a child.

Yet they ignored me and ordered a final hearing. I did my research and used the money from one of my book payments to hire one of the best barristers in Exeter – just short of four thousand pounds for the day. Josh and I travelled to her chambers in Exeter and we spent hours going through the trial bundle with her. She just kept rolling her eyes, asking herself why the hell they had sent this to a final hearing. It was bizarre.

At the final hearing, my barrister went off to meet with his in a private room. She came back ten minutes later and said they were going to ask together that the hearing was cancelled. Betsy's dad agreed to apologise for the voicemails he'd left her, and both barristers felt it was pointless dragging it out any further.

We all went into court, and the magistrates agreed it could be cancelled. We were there less than an hour and I was almost four thousand pounds down.

We waited for the court order which was decided in another hearing. By this point Betsy had turned sixteen so could no longer be included in the matters. It was all now about Tallulah.

The worst Christmas

It was agreed contact could be letters and cards once a month with gifts sent on birthdays and at Christmas.

We received the first letter to Tallulah at the beginning of November. It was a card in which he said he had begun breeding dogs. He asked her if she wanted one of his puppies then enclosed printed photographs of the mum and dad dogs to show her what they would look like. I wanted to kill. Of course she wanted a fucking puppy. She's seen the parents who were fluffy and white and cute. What child wouldn't want a puppy? It just left me raging because she was so upset and confused.

He sent nothing for Betsy.

We then didn't hear anything until he sent someone to deliver presents on the doorstep at 8 p.m. on Christmas Eve 2020. There was a whole bag of presents for Tallulah, a fifty-pound JD Sports voucher and a card.

There was nothing for Betsy.

That was possibly the worst Christmas we've ever had since we left him, if I'm honest. Tallulah opened the presents and card, and I could see she didn't know how to feel or what to say about the content of the card.

Betsy was feeling so many emotions, even though she kept saying she didn't want anything. She was annoyed that Tallulah had opened his presents and asked her if she was going to keep them. Tallulah didn't know if she wanted to keep them and then Betsy lost it. I got it; I got every single bit of feeling she had that she had been abandoned and rejected whilst her sister was being showered in love.

Betsy then felt overwhelming guilt that she had lost it with her little sister about Christmas gifts. Within half an hour of those presents being delivered on Christmas Eve I had both girls beside themselves. Tallulah was sobbing that Betsy didn't get any presents and she felt guilty she had opened hers. She was also then really worried that she might upset her dad and ruin his Christmas if she returned them all to him but felt she should so it was fair on Betsy. Betsy refused to come out of her room, sobbing so hard she couldn't catch her breath but she didn't know why she was so upset. She couldn't make any sense of her emotions nor could she regulate them.

I realised I couldn't do anything to make either of them better, because there's no cure for a narcissistic parent — sometimes you just have to ride it out and that's what they did. They spent Christmas Eve alone in their rooms, crying too many tears over a situation that should never have been allowed to happen by professionals whose job it is to protect children when their parents can't. I read his Christmas card: 'To Tallulah, I'll become the person and the father you deserve. Will write again in January. Love you all the world, Dad xxxx.'

He didn't write again in January, or February. He didn't send her a birthday card or present that March. In fact, since 24 December 2020 neither of the girls saw or heard anything, until, really weirdly, at 2 a.m. on 25 September 2022. I woke up to Betsy calling me, frantic, from a night-club where he was sat at the next table to her and she didn't know what to do. I told her to leave and I would drive over and get her, but he spotted her. As she walked down the stairs he put his hand on her shoulder and said, 'Wahhhhhhey,' like he had just spotted an old, long-lost friend, then he walked off.

It makes my brain ache to think that he dragged us through court for two years, that he spent thousands of pounds hiring the best solicitor and barristers, left voice notes and sent texts to us saying how he couldn't wait to see me in court and how was going to 'win' and 'get the girls' and 'destroy me'. When he didn't, when he couldn't – because his own actions destroyed it for him – he just stopped trying. He could have written every single month, he could have sent cards and photos and gifts and books. He could have gone and got therapy, worked on his anger and he could have tried, every single month, to show the girls he had changed, for them. The reality – as I see every single day – is that it stopped being about spending time with them, being a dad to them; it became about him fighting me. It felt like it was all about trying to have some control over me through family court. And then, when he was given an olive branch to rebuild trust with his daughters, to work hard and show the girls he could change and be a better person, he didn't do it.

Yet being around those girls is one of my most happy places. The banter between them, the way we all laugh until we cry at the most stupid stuff, the way they love – they have so much love to give, they love so ridiculously hard, and he just walked away from that like it wasn't there. They are the air in my world. If they were taken away from me I'd struggle to breathe without them, but he lives really well without them in his life so, you know, I have to accept it. I have to remember they have a stable home, they are surrounded by love and they will be OK and actually it's his loss. Having them in my world shows me how much he will be suffering without them, even if he has chosen to deny that.

After Betsy saw him in the nightclub, she told me she's fine, that seeing him for the first time in five years hasn't upset her. I think about my own dad, who I haven't spoken to for twelve years. While driving, I have given way to him in his van several times and I saw him once queuing for an ice cream at the beach and I can't work out if he doesn't recognise me or he pretends not to. I also wonder if it would feel worse for me if he did wave or smile. Probably, I imagine, it would be.

I remember when I started my Patreon account and I was chatting to my followers on the private Instagram account I have for them and my mum called to say, 'I have some bad news. Your dad's been rushed into hospital with chest pains and he's in a bad way.' I instantly cut off the Instagram Story I was recording but it had uploaded. I was so preoccupied I wasn't really thinking but when I went on my account later I had so many messages from people who were advising me to go to the hospital and see my dad before it was too late. They were saying things like, 'You only get one parent,' and reminding me that when he's gone he's gone and it will be too late to change the way things are.

There wasn't one part of me that wanted to reach out to him, even knowing he was in pain and it could be life-threatening. Does that make me a bad person? I don't think so, because I have to work so hard to be a good mum. I have to try and raise my children to the best of my ability, but also I have to be the best version of me, knowing that children are products of their environment. I also have to mop up my shit when I make mistakes, I have to own my bad choices and apologise to the kids when I get things wrong. I don't merely think I'm a mum because they're my children. You're not just entitled to be a parent – you have to work hard at that role. When my dad was rushed to hospital and I was told to expect the worst I felt sorry for him. I looked at that situation and thought how I would hate to be on my deathbed having no relationship with some of my children and the majority of my grandchildren. What a fucking shitshow to think, Is this it?, while knowing you haven't earned that father or grand-father badge.

Even when I read the messages from people telling me to go visit him I wasn't tempted, because my children deserve better, they deserve a figure who wants to show up for them, who loves them unconditionally. They've never had that in him. I am his daughter, I am his child and he should be committed to being my dad for his whole life, no matter what, but you can't force that. You cannot make an alcoholic stop drinking or a gambler stop gambling; they have to want to do that and it's the same with a parent. It's one of the toughest, most difficult, relentless jobs in the world and some men and women are just not cut out for it. I cannot make my dad want to be my dad, the same as Betsy and Tallulah can't with theirs. Either way it isn't a good feeling. It hurts having a father who can't love and prioritise you the way you deserve and need. It fucking wrecks your heart and it leaves you questioning so much, and if it doesn't hurt that much, it is only because you've normalised it, in order to be able to cope and get through life.

And with Betsy and Tallulah I'm here to help them to try and navigate their way through life. I get what they feel because I feel it all too and some days it sucks.

Betsy went on to finish college, reluctantly whilst contin-uing to work hard at her other jobs. To date we have had one result for psychology. She got a merit, so it was worth doing perhaps, who knows? She currently has no idea what she wants to do or where she wants to be.

When I pick life apart and when I delve into my past and I look around at my friends' journeys I see that we're in such a hurry to 'get there'. But actually, where is 'there'?

I started my children at preschool full time at the age of three, two of my August babies went into reception and began learning when they had just turned four.

Four. Years. Old.

That is less than a year away for Wilby now and they were in education full-time.

They learn from such a young age. They're in a structured environment from being babies and when they are a teenager they choose their core subjects. They're under such pressure to gain the results they need to go to college, then they are off to uni or they get an apprenticeship to get a job. From there they work, full-time and hard, before they're expected to settle and pay bills and take full responsibility for their lives and maybe the lives of tiny humans that so many people in society still expect them to create.

It's mind-blowing. Like, where is their fun? Where is 'their time?' The time to just sit and think about what they want? The time to have fun, make memories and mistakes without a whole world of responsibilities and burdens sat on their shoulders? How are they supposed to choose what they want to do with their lives when they have no time to go and live them, to experience things and meet people and see places without a constant worry of what they should be doing?

Right now, Betsy is there. She has some friends who have a life plan, are set on becoming midwives or criminal lawyers and are starting uni with a goal. She has another friend who's joined the RAF and, as incredible as that is, most of them honestly don't have a fucking clue about what they want to be or where they want to go. What I find really sad is many of them have no options, because they are told by their parents what uni they'll be going to and what course they'll be studying to get the career they are expected to have. And maybe they're right, maybe the pushy parents who force their kids to do stuff to ensure they become a success and earn a decent wage are the ones who are right. Maybe I'm wrong – but for now I'm OK with being wrong. I'm OK with Betsy having no plan or clue about what she wants to do with her life. I'm happy to support her to go travel the world, alone. To save her wages to then board a plane and fly to Thailand, to meet people from all over the world and make memories she will never get in Torbay. But I am also as happy to support her if she doesn't do that.

I don't care whether my daughter earns tens of thousands of pounds in a career that sounds glorious on paper that I can tell all my friends about and I don't care if she pulls pints in a local pub for the minimum wage. I care that she's happy, I care that she's loved and she loves and I care that she's OK, because this world can be brutal and cruel and it can eat you up. As we see time and time again, having a successful career, glistening exam results or a huge income doesn't protect you from those things.

The plan is for her to keep working and keep saving.

She currently does three days a week at the Patchwork Store, where the feedback I get from customers on how smiley, sweet and chatty she is warms my soul weekly. She then has a second job in a restaurant and she pings me her wages to hold back and spends her tips, which are incredible some nights.

Last week she went to Liverpool to stay with family friends for the weekend and she has decided to move there, to just live the city life for a while, to get a full-time job, meet some new friends and see what excites her. She may get homesick quickly and return but I have a feeling she will fall in love with all the different parts of the world and the people in it. I remind her constantly that I could have never planned to do the job I finally became successful at because we were made to sit and plan our futures when the internet wasn't even a thing.

We never know what's coming for us. We don't know what's out there that we can't yet see and it's pointless forcing yourself into something unless you feel passion like fire in your belly. Yes, we may have to stick at jobs we hate because we have bills to pay. I've done this throughout my life, but that doesn't mean we should ever stop planning or dreaming about what we do want 'one day'. We should never write it off by convincing ourselves it's too hard or impossible to achieve. It's all about mindset and situations.

Betsy and I haven't fought since that day over her college. I mean, I call her and kick off when she robs my hair straighteners or concealer or she calls me and kicks off when Tallulah robs her new leggings or trainers, but we haven't made either of us feel unwell, there have been no cross words or raised voices and I really hope it continues. That last fight taught me so much about the parent I never want to be . . . it also made me think really hard about the education system and how we value success.

What we don't teach our kids in school

The last few years of school weren't easy for Seb, Josh and me and they're quickly becoming difficult for both Lula and Isaac.

All three of them had some lessons and teachers they just didn't like. Seb chose business studies in year nine but instantly detested it. But he wasn't allowed to drop it and I don't think that subject was particularly pleasurable for him or his teacher.

Covid hit in the most important years of Betsy and Seb's lives schooling-wise because they were in their final years – she had her GCSEs cancelled. I think Seb was expecting the same. I certainly was, considering he had missed so much time with his school being closed. He spent two years in limbo and the ups and downs of it all certainly took its toll. It was a time when both were transitioning – emotionally, mentally and physically at such a rapid rate. It would be tough anyway but then to have all this on top was almost impossible to cope with.

I now have five children in the education system. Betsy has just left and I feel this is a really important topic for me to cover. It's one I get asked about all the time.

We got called in for meetings with Seb's head of year last year when he returned after Covid and before he sat his GCSEs. The head of year told us that Seb spent most of his lessons with his head on the desk, not engaging. He was late to lessons and showed no passion or keenness to learn. When we spoke to Seb about this he agreed, but his argument is that he is met by certain teachers who immediately bark orders at him and shout when his laptop doesn't have enough charge or he doesn't have the right pen. They don't use his name when they speak to him and send him to isolation before they've even given him time to offer any kind of explanation for what he's being punished for.

This is something I have been arguing about for years. It's pointless – because neither party wins. The teacher isn't teaching and the child isn't learning and I imagine both of them feel pretty fucked off at the situation. I ask the school why certain teachers don't just approach him differently, like, 'Hey, Seb! Good weekend, bud? Tell me something you've enjoyed getting up to.' This to be followed up with, 'Right, guys, let's get our Chromebooks out and crack on,' (to the whole class, rather than just to one child).

I'm told that this can't be done because Seb's attitude is consistently bad. But for more than eight years now I don't think there's anyone who's seen the hard parts of Seb more than me, not even Josh. I have been the one to wake him and put him to bed every day and care for him and he is never ever instantly horrible to me. That's because he's met with, 'Hey, babe, you OK? Good day?' And a hug. And that's just it. We are the adults. I am the adult and a teacher is the adult and it's up to us to be the bigger person and be respectful in order for the children to copy that behaviour. A child is a product of their environment. Seb would be hard-pushed to walk in the door from school and start gobbling off at me when I greet him in the way I always have done. Instead, he gives me a hug and a kiss and tells me about his day. Sometimes he's in a shit mood or he's quiet and heads straight for his room but that's also OK because some days I'm the same. It's normal for our children to feel a range of emotions. We shouldn't expect them to be happy and smiley and respectful twenty-four-seven because guess what? We're not.

Now, if I instantly ordered him to clean his room or take his bag and shoes off without saying 'Hello' or didn't use his name when I spoke to him he would probably behave the same way he does at school. And why shouldn't he? If he's met with an adult shouting and ordering him around, why isn't he going to be confrontational? It's like catching a child being violent and smacking them as a punishment. It literally makes no sense. And what good is that for anyone? It just leaves people feeling shit and confuses children.

The second thing that grates is when I speak to older generations about the education system needing to move with the times, and I'm met with, 'He's lucky he wasn't at school when I was or he would have got the slipper or the cane off the teacher,' or, 'If I'd have gone into school and answered back to a teacher the way they do now my dad would have battered me when I got home.' It's exhausting – just because years ago it was deemed acceptable to be beaten by your teacher or your parents, it doesn't mean it was ever OK. For a child to live in fear of an adult is not acceptable, because ultimately adults can be awful humans. A small minority of teachers can and will clearly dislike children, just as some will favour others. It blows my mind that once upon a time we allowed these people to have the authority to physically hurt a child with a piece of wood, a shoe or their hands.

As much as the secondary school my kids attend has been incredible they still occasionally do stuff, as do many other schools, that also blow my brain. Their rules are two warnings and then the child gets isolation. The warnings are for things like forgetting a piece of equipment, not having the correct uniform, having a bad attitude or not being willing to learn etc. Both our boys get isolated monthly, sometimes weekly and occasionally daily.

If a child is coming from an unsafe home because they live with abuse, neglect or in poverty, then remembering to bring a pen or finding their tie is the least of their worries. To then be punished for this is just insane. Teachers tell me they make exceptions for vulnerable families or certain situations and my closing argument is this: what about the families that we don't see? What about the families we think are healthy and positive? What about the children who we are punishing who aren't red-flagging?

Look at the case of siblings Luke, Ryan and Charlotte Hart. They were raised by their parents together and were all grade-A students at school. Charlotte went on to uni to train to become a midwife and both boys got jobs out of the country as engineers. In 2016 the boys learned that their dad had murdered their mum and younger sister by shooting them dead in a swimming pool car park before turning the gun on himself.

Everyone who knew this family was in shock. Nobody could believe the news, including former teachers and ex-pupils of their school. And I can guarantee the majority of you don't know about this case. Why? Why have we not rammed it down people's throats to show the reality of how domestic abuse happens and how easy it is to not be seen? I know why, because the headlines were too busy victim-blaming. They said a 'family man' lost control, focusing on the 'poor-me' suicide note he took the time to write before he murdered two innocent victims. We don't know about it because the media don't portray the reality behind it. And that is still very much the reality of hidden domestic abuse.

Children don't turn up to school with a flashing beacon that shows they're living with a perpetrator and being subjected to abuse in their home. They often present as grade-A students, quiet and hardworking, sometimes shy. They have clean uniform and hair that smells of strawberry shampoo. Just as Luke and Ryan Hart had, yet they, alongside their mum and sister had been subjected to domestic abuse all their lives. Their father had total control over their entire family and not only did no one spot it, they spent the majority of their upbringing not recognising what it was because the awareness just isn't there. The boys now dedicate their lives to going round the world and educating people on the devastation domestic abuse has and how to recognise the early signs.

I feel like the world has moved at such a rapid speed, yet the education system still focuses on kids leaving with nothing but their GCSEs. When they prep for their exams they are offered extra revision clubs to ensure they get the best grades possible and we encourage them as children to map out their entire future. At the age of thirteen they're choosing core subjects to study, then we're asking where they are heading in regard to college, uni or apprenticeships. I feel like we still miss so much of the important stuff. We still don't focus enough on the most important things that can alter their entire futures – safe sex, consent, healthy relationships and understanding domestic abuse and addiction. We don't teach them how to manage money or why their brains may feel the way they do because of the changes going on within their bodies.

We still don't teach them the importance of manners and respecting others and themselves. We don't teach them what the consequences are if they're bullying others – the proper consequences, that they don't often see. We don't make it easy enough for them to access help and support if they are being bullied. I know so many of my friends' children who don't feel they have relationships with any teachers they can trust. Children go into adulthood unaware they've been raised in an abusive household or lived with an addicted parent. They think having a parent who perpetrates abuse or drinks daily to function is totally normal. I know this because I work with women every week who have been or are still going through this. They enter into each new relationship, going from perpetrator to perpetrator because they were raised by them. It's what they grow up to think is normal to look for in men.

Why aren't we teaching children what a healthy, positive relationship looks like? If children aren't taught they have the absolute right to say 'No' when they're being pressured or forced into having sex, how will they know they can? We are currently dealing with some of the worst cases of domestic abuse within teenage relationships at school. It's real and it destroys childhoods. So many kids are going through this stuff and if they're not they one hundred per cent know someone within their school who is. I work with women who have made some really bad choices as a teenager or a young adult, myself included, and all of them say, 'If only I'd have known,' or, 'If only someone had told me.'

Parents often don't tell their kids stuff. They either don't think it's necessary or they don't know how to approach it. When I post certain things on social media (for instance, when I discuss period pants in front of my kids) I'm met with a huge flurry of messages from women who cringe at the thought of talking to their daughters about starting their periods. They have no clue how to raise it, what to say or what to do. It's really sad, for both them and their child, because it's one of the most natural things we go through in life. If a parent can't talk to their daughter about what happens when she starts her period then she certainly isn't going to be able to sit down and warn them about the horrors that come with unprotected sex, the issues around consent or being of an age where you can emotionally cope with the feelings you get with being sexually active. This is why it absolutely needs to be taught in schools. Not just a day's sex education where you look at a slide show of a womb and an egg, or a teacher slides a condom onto a banana to show a classroom full of cringing kids how to have safe sex. No.

It's the same for the kids who have no one, the ones we both see and don't see. When I go and watch my kids' school plays, attend their leavers' assembly or go to an open afternoon to see their work displayed, they race to find me. I see their eyes darting around everywhere when they're on stage in a donkey costume and when they spot me the relief I see in them is heartwarming. I recently did a podcast with an incredible guy called Josh Connelly, who said, 'What about all the kids that look out from the stage and there's no one there? What about the kids that don't even bother looking out any more because they've never had anyone come to see them at anything?'

All it takes, for a child that comes from a broken or unsafe home, is one person to care for them. I will cover it more later on, but I know this because I was the child from the broken home who was lucky enough to have a form tutor who believed me, who called children's services and saved me. But there are hundreds of thousands of children like this today, looking out at you waving to your child on stage. You just don't see them because you're not looking for them, you're looking at your child.

Why in schools do we not just employ good, kind people or even have a volunteer scheme in place? Just for adults to come, to sit in an office with an open door, to wander around the school throughout the day and get to know the kids.

This week I called a meeting at Isaac's school after one of his teachers sent home a long email about his behaviour not being great in lessons. The head of year was there and, as the meeting finished, he said to Isaac, 'Remember how lucky you are to have this meeting, because we haven't called it, your parents have. Your parents wanted to give up their time to come here and talk to us to make sure we can work with you so you're happy and you're doing OK. They're here because they want the very best for you. There are so many kids in this school that don't have that. Some children don't have anyone that would ever sit in a meeting for them so don't forget how incredible it is that you have that support.'

It broke me.

We forget that, just because we ask our kids how their day was when they get in each night, we make them a decent dinner and ensure their bedding smells fresh, that some kids don't have that. Some kids go home to empty cupboards and sleep on a mattress with no bedding that they wet each night and some kids have never ever had a parent ask how their day was. So imagine, when they walked from one lesson to another, they were met by someone who was kind and smiley, who knew their name and their likes and interests, who stopped and asked them if they scored a goal in their last game of football or how the bread tasted that they baked in food tech. What if girls could pop to an office and ask for sanitary products with no judgement? At home they may have to use wads of tissue as their mum has no money. What if those special staff or volunteers sat in on the school assemblies and leavers' presentations? When those children can't see a parent they instead could spot the staff, and would be met with the same wave and smile as all their peers.

Instead, we just ignore all of the shit stuff that so many kids are enduring. We need the real life, nitty-gritty, soul-destroying parts of childhood to form part of the curriculum – not just in a 'We do cover it' way I get from some teachers or schools I've asked but in a 'It's taught daily' way. In a 'we really care' way. It would become normal, giving kids the courage to recognise their home life isn't OK and they would be more likely to speak up. It would mean there are fewer STDs and teenage pregnancies because kids would actually be fully educated and feel in control of their bodies and decisions.

Raising awareness of everything I've just mentioned needs to be as important as achieving your GCSEs. Ultimately, it doesn't matter if you finish school with the best grades. If you don't have awareness of the things that can destroy your life or the lives of others then a handful of GCSEs mean absolutely nothing in the long run.

Taking on the toughest conversations

I spoke in the last book about how damaged Seb was in the first few years when he came to live with Josh and me. As a result of family court proceedings, certain criteria had to be met by their mum before the boys visited her. Things started red-flagging again in autumn 2017 after having over six really positive months where they saw her weekly and stayed overnight a few times. Josh called me one afternoon to say she had called the police to say she needed them to send Josh. Josh wouldn't go, but we felt she was vulnerable. I could still tell he was worried. I went and picked his mum up and drove to the boys' mother's house so I wasn't by myself. Josh's mum had been like a mother to her for years whilst they were together and tried to stay in her life after they split to support her. Despite everything, she still knew, for the boys, we should go.

We arrived. Out of respect for the boys, I won't go into detail about what happened.

At the same time, her boyfriend arrived. She then began to get really upset. We decided it was best we leave. I remember thinking how unwell those few hours left me feeling. The whole scenario buzzed in my head, it consumed me. I would wake in the night from dreams about it and it left me feeling so out of sorts.

It was at that point I realised Seb had endured that for over a year after Josh had left. All the stuff he had confided about how he was a victim of a homelife that could be chaotic, and it caused him real stress. I was struggling to process it as a middle-aged woman with life experience. I couldn't imagine how he dealt with it all when he was just eight years old.

The next day she called me to apologise. I saw her regularly after that. I would take her shopping and run errands. I would always take a friend with me, usually my best friend Lianne, or Josh's mum. Mainly because some days she still worried me.

On the last time the boys stayed with her, 18 October 2017, an incident occurred. Josh and I were on my first tour date in Birmingham. Josh's mum went to collect Seb and called us. After that Seb made the decision he didn't want to see her again and we fully supported him and she accepted it without question.

Josh arranged to drop Isaac at 11 a.m. one day after Christmas so they could exchange gifts and soon after he arrived, he called me and he was crying. He just assumed because she hadn't seen Isaac for almost two months, she would now be in a position to care for him. Josh had got Isaac out of the car. It became clear as Isaac was hugging his mum that she was not well enough to take care of them. Josh then had to tell Isaac he couldn't stay.

I can't imagine doing that. I hate that he had to do that. I hate that he had to be the bad one. The one to tell a seven-year-old little boy who had just greeted his mummy and was excited to open his Christmas presents, and give her presents that we had wrapped with him, that less than a minute after arriving he now wouldn't be staying. He was strapped back into the car, Josh shut the door and then he rang me whilst he leaned against the boot so Isaac couldn't see or hear him. He couldn't hold it together. I couldn't hold it together. I told him to drive home and we would try, together, to somehow sort it out.

I remember Seb raging when I got off the phone to Josh. He was sat on the stairs listening to our call. We found him so many times over those years sat on those stairs listening to so many calls and conversations. He was already upset that we were sending Isaac that day.

That day with Isaac, for Seb, it looked like we were just going to allow the same thing to happen to his little brother and it appeared to him that we weren't recognising or believing what he had gone through, because as he (quite rightly) stated, 'If you had, why would you ever send Isaac to her alone without anyone to protect him?' Seb had spent too much time protecting Isaac when his mum couldn't; he had cleaned Isaac up after he had been to the toilet and he had heated his bottles of milk. Once he had even tried to make them Super Noodles but he put the foil packet in the microwave, causing a fire. He had to call the neighbour for help. All of these things he had kept secret for so long and then he came to confide in us. Now he had to watch us continue to send his baby brother without anyone there to look out for him.

The thing is, when you're in this situation, with such tiny children, and you have a court order stating they have to have contact with the other parent, you don't know what to do for the best. It's all confusing and hard and it's daunting. Ultimately, all Josh ever wanted for the boys was for them to have both him and their mum giving them the love and security they needed and deserved.

We made a decision that day, on 6 January 2018, after all four of us shed too many tears, felt too many emotions and Josh and I were just at a loss as to how to do things for the best. I'm not going into the specific issues we were dealing with, but every decision about contact was only done to help the boys feel safer and less anxious. Josh and I agreed that, unless she could focus on their needs, Isaac wouldn't visit again. Emotionally, at that point, the damage to him was nowhere near as much as Seb had suffered, and the further harm Josh and I were causing Seb by sending Isaac by himself was unfair. It was about acknowledging what we felt was best and safest for Isaac. Seb also felt angry at Isaac that he still wanted to see his mum. We explained to Seb that Isaac had totally different memories and experiences with their mum and we felt at that time Isaac was too tiny to have to hear what Seb had experienced.

Josh engaged with experts and supportive charitable organisations, who told him he needed to be honest with the boys but to explain it to them in an age-appropriate way. By not talking about it, they said it created an elephant in the room and the damage to the boys would be worse.

I remember Josh explaining the facts to Isaac as they had guided him, just the same way that I can picture the scene after my mum left. I was sat in the lounge at our old house, perched on the edge of our brown corner sofa and Josh went into the boys' room opposite. It was just Isaac in there. Seb was playing out with his friends in the road. Isaac was lying on his bottom bunk playing with his Moshi Monsters figures. He looks so tiny when I picture it now. Josh told him that he wouldn't be seeing his mum again for a while. It was heartbreaking, because Isaac just didn't get it. He kept asking if we could take her some treats so he could see her again. He wanted reassurance over who was looking after her.

I genuinely don't think anything had affected Josh more than having to deliver those difficult words to Isaac and make those decisions as best as he could.

Watching the process was pretty soul-destroying until the boys accepted it and we realised that conversation massively helped the situation. Isaac was tearful and still sad, whilst Seb was full of anger and hate. Them coming together, sharing a bedroom and ultimately grieving for their mum whilst feeling different emotions at totally different ages was really fucking difficult.

I understood because, once upon a time, as a four-year-old girl, my amazing mum disappeared one day and never came back, only I was never told anything and no one ever stepped in and made anything feel better. And not only did no one give me any answers, they didn't acknowledge it was happening. I look back and think, How was I ever supposed to process and grieve over a forbidden topic? I must have had so many feelings pent up inside and it's no wonder I made some of the choices I did when I hit my teens. Not one other person around me seemed to recognise what was happening, not even my siblings who were going through it alongside me.

I was just left to navigate my childhood consumed by feelings of abandonment and rejection and I would rather cut my own arm off than let that be repeated by any child I know. I swooped in, because they needed me to. I ensured their mum was only spoken about in a positive way. It's unbelievable the number of people, with absolutely no awareness, who we would bump into and who would say, 'Are they still seeing their mum?' in a stage whisper. It just created further upset and trauma. Seb would still get so angry he couldn't contain it and he would have a rant or a cry and he didn't care who was there – that was difficult when Isaac was present. I had to remind Seb to be mindful of that whilst still ensuring I was validating his feelings.

I had to revisit everything I felt when I lost *my* mum and, as we see everywhere in society, your mother is one of the most prominent figures for us. If I could have gone back to being a child I would have wanted people to talk about her. I wouldn't have wanted to hear negative, horrible things about her – even if the person saying those things believed they were true. I didn't need to hear it. I would have wanted to have been able to tell the people caring for me when I was thinking of her, missing her. I would have wanted them to have loved me through that, to reassure me and let me know my feelings were always OK. So that's what I did for Seb and Isaac and it's what I still do today.

I was brimming with thoughts and feelings that I couldn't make any sense of and a lot of the time they felt overwhelming. In the podcast I spoke about earlier we talked about children not having important things explained to them. I suppose my dad didn't know how to have that conversation with his four-year-old daughter. By the time I was the age at which I could understand what he was trying to explain, we had gone so many years acting like the situation wasn't happening it was probably even harder for him to raise it. That might have been why he just totally ignored it.

This was the weirdest fucking decision for me as a child. I'd had a devoted, incredible mum for the first (almost) five years of my life. I woke up to find she'd just left, then she moved away and I saw her around three times a year, yet still no one told me anything and neither did she when I saw her. It just became normal that she just wasn't there any more. Only it wasn't normal, it was fucking horrific. It was the stuff of nightmares to lose a parent, yet to have everyone continue like this was all normal. I felt at times like I was going mental. I went from being a confused young child into being an absolutely raging teenager who hated the world and I just wanted to get off my face, forget it all and feel loved by the most inappropriate people.

So when Seb and Isaac experienced a similar situation, I revisited some of the worst parts of my past to grasp how best it was to get through, to think about what I needed and wanted all those years ago. I realised that, more than anything, I want all my kids to question stuff, I want them to know they can ask Josh and me anything that confuses or upsets them and I want them to know it's OK to grieve and miss things and people, no matter what — or who. There is never any shame or guilt in that.

The boys rarely mention their mum now and some-times I will bring her up, asking them if they miss her, if they've thought of her or want to discuss anything. Seb always gets irritated with me for asking and shuts me down. Isaac always says 'No,' but in a calmer, quieter way. I have to be prepared that one day she may reach out to them and that may or may not be a good thing depending on the content of the message and how stable she is at that point. That's the reality of children growing up – I've come to understand you can't protect them for ever and sometimes you can only try and cushion the blow when it comes.

Back when Josh first delivered that news to the boys I felt they needed him around. They needed him to help them make sense of the huge changes they were going through. At the same time, we were tens of thousands of pounds in debt. For us to survive Josh had to work overtime all over the country, sometimes for weeks at a time, but right then the boys needed stability and love. They needed to test their boundaries and know they were safe. They needed to know that, no matter what, they had a home, a dad and a step-mum who were going to do everything in their power to fix all their broken bits and help them to heal.

There were no more texts, calls or lengthy messages once they lived with us permanently. Their mum just accepted it was for the best at that time. It's now been almost five years since the boys have seen her. In that time we've received some voicemails, texts and once a call from a withheld number.

It's sad. She has missed out on five years of the boys' lives. They are the funniest, most beautiful boys and, when I watch them transition as they have, into secondary school or getting their first job and when we watched Seb go to prom, I couldn't help but think it's such a great loss. It's never not in my thoughts, because they came from her – she grew them inside her, she birthed them, and I just don't understand how we're here, but it is the way it is and that's not because of Josh and me alienating her as a parent. Nobody can make someone be a parent. Maybe the longer she goes without seeing or speaking to them the harder it must be for her to reach out. I don't know. Five years is a huge amount of time not to see your children.

When Seb came to live with us, he couldn't cope if Josh and I had a drink together because he needed one of us to be in control.

He was in this heightened state of alert at all times. He rarely slept and the slightest noise would wake him if he did. When he was awake he was wide-eyed and constantly looking out for the negative, bad and dangerous stuff.

I often worried what kind of teenager he would be because of it, we all did, when it came to an age where he watched his friends try a cigarette or alcohol, but actually he's OK now. At the age of almost seventeen his worries and fears totally disappeared. I wonder if that's because he's spent so many years seeing people around him being responsible or if it's just an age thing. Curiosity and/or peer pressure gets the better of you and you just stop caring as much. I hope that being away from the negative stuff has helped him come to terms with some of his trauma.

On the whole, he is the best boy!

He's kind and respectful and he idolises his siblings. He and Betsy are the best of friends and, when the shit hits the fan at school for Lula or Isaac, he sorts it without question, even when they've made bad choices. He's not made any decisions that have kept Josh and me up for days on end or made us question if we've failed as parents. Yes, he's doing stuff that makes us worry a little but he's as responsible as can be. He wears protection when he has sex and I've taken him to the sexual health clinic after his relationships have ended to get full check-ups and he's absolutely fine with doing this, because he's mature enough to know he's taking responsibility for himself and other people. He occasionally smokes weed or drinks alcohol, but he tells me so I can arrange for him to get home safely. He knows I know he's OK and I don't worry. Over the last five years I have had so many kids come to our home who lie to their parents. I see their jaws drop when my kids tell me they're going to a party where they might smoke a joint or ask me to grab more condoms when I go shopping.

Yes, I wish the kids never felt the need to vape or try drugs and in an ideal world they'd have sex with the one person they end up with. But this isn't an ideal world. It's messy and brutal and it's full of highs then lows, so I need them to know I will never judge them. Of course they've made decisions that have made my heart feel heavy. They've lost friends because of their actions and they're not always kind, considerate or hardworking, but life is about learning. It's about achieving incredible things and educating yourself through your worst fuck-ups. I'm here to guide and steer them and hope they make more good choices than bad, and I pray the bad ones aren't so bad we can't work through them together. They have to be free to make their own choices.

I don't believe we should control our children to the point they're too scared to do stuff or are too scared to tell us. Our kids know I won't get mad or upset because it's likely they're never going to make as many poor decisions as I did when I was their age. They're going to treat people much better than I ever did. Once upon a time, I was a pretty broken teenager who made some shit decisions and hurt a lot of good people. I had no adult to properly confide in and I feel like I've turned out OK.

Hopefully, them trying to navigate their way through life with Josh and me behind them to ensure they're all right will mean they'll be fine. It's what any of us want for our kids at the end of the day. It's hard to know what's right and what you should be doing. We're all just trying our best and it's absolutely OK that we do it differently to one another.

5

SECONDARY SCHOOL TRANSITIONS

Isaac has always been the easiest. By far. Until September 2021.

He went to primary school without issues and worked well whilst he was there. He was so laidback and chilled and he formed good friendships. Even when things went wrong (for instance, once he came home with a huge black eye where his mate had punched him) he just told us, 'He's having a tough time' and I felt so proud of Isaac for seeing this. Isaac made friends with him again the next day and held no grudge. He's always just got on with stuff and naively I expected that to continue.

He started year seven at the same time Lula joined his school in year eight. For the first term he was his usual, well-behaved self and he really enjoyed it. Soon after he began getting detentions, then getting isolated and his class charts made for a grim read. If you haven't yet experienced class charts, these take the form of a huge circle on an app that shows your child's progress and behaviour. Green means good, red means not good. (Again, I really hate this system on behalf of the kids who are trying to get green when their worlds are falling apart behind the scenes.) Isaac's class chart was soon pretty much red most days and his warnings fast began to outweigh his merits. I called it the 'wheel of doom'. Because it really was in our house most of the time!

When Betsy and Seb began secondary school they had out-of-school clubs they went to which took up a lot of their time. Betsy trained at gymnastics twelve hours a week and Seb was a semi-pro footballer. He trained evenings and played all over the country, both Saturday and Sunday, every week. Although Lula didn't have an out-of-school interest as such, she was just trying to survive in year seven. She didn't have solid friendship groups and still spent her time hanging out with her family and pets. I knew her whereabouts and she didn't get herself into trouble.

Isaac had always liked the thought of joining clubs, but we've tried most things and he loses interest after a few weeks, no matter how much we encourage him. The issue I think is that this was the first time we had a child who had started secondary school with 'time'. He had time to hang out with friends because he didn't have any other commitments. His new friends had some nights when they had clubs which meant he would then skip between friendship groups. He was meeting all kinds of different people and trying to fit in with them all. He also had the pressure of being Seb's little brother. Seb by this point was in year eleven and was I suppose quite popular (another thing about school I detest is the ranking of how cool kids are).

Isaac started making some really bad choices. Choices that I think felt worse because until then Isaac had never, ever caused any issues or problems so we just couldn't understand where it was coming from. Within weeks of him starting school he got beaten up twice, both by older kids. The first time a group of kids he didn't know were smoking in the park and a mum and toddler arrived so he shouted at them to stop smoking. It was actually quite sad, and sweet, because he didn't want the baby to be around people smoking and felt sorry for the mum. Josh pointed out it wasn't Isaac's place to dish out rules in a public place, and he reminded him he isn't the 'park warden'.

He was then caught on camera in the background, laughing, when another one of his friends smashed up a school laptop all over the road and pavement. The video made its way to us, the school and around town. When we spoke to him about it he just kept saying he hadn't done anything wrong. We explained that if one child beats another child up and his group of mates stand by and encourage it, find it amusing or don't intervene, they're equally as guilty.

I went through his phone and found videos of him vaping and swearing. I read messages to find he was not being very nice to others in large group chats and, on the whole, he was totally unrecognisable as the Isaac we knew and loved.

We put measures in place to try and monitor his behaviour. He would do really well so we would give him more freedom and then he would totally ruin it for himself again straight away, leaving us questioning where we'd gone wrong. We were getting calls from other kids' parents about his involvement in incidents. He was getting isolated regularly at school and then he got a serious sanction for a fight that happened. Every time we tried to talk, he would lose his temper and scream and shout at us through tears, then run upstairs and trash his room. He would totally deny any involvement. When he couldn't deny one fight because there was CCTV evidence, he just kept saying the other kid deserved it and the CCTV hadn't caught the provocation.

Honestly, my head was blown.

Seb and Betsy tried to talk to him. Josh tried the firm approach and took everything off him and made him be a part of the family much more. Yet it felt unfair to make him hang out with his two-year-old brother at soft play and toddler-splash pools when all his friends were out doing fun stuff.

I sat down and had a huge chat with him.

He never mentions his mum so I made the decision to bring her up. I asked him if he wanted to know anything, if he had any questions. He said, 'I don't even remember what she looks like,' but this was followed by so many tears of anger and confusion. Ultimately, it isn't normal to grow up with mum absent. Not many of his friends are in similar situations. Isaac has stability and love from Josh and me, but I am a hundred per cent sure he has questions.

After my mum disappeared, I was left with so many feelings I didn't understand and so many unanswered questions I couldn't make any sense of. Abandonment and rejection in childhood by a parent fucks you up for life, no matter how much love surrounds you. I don't care what anyone says. To have one of the two people who chose to bring you into this world walk away without explanation leaves you feeling like you were never enough. You may be OK for a while, but one day you'll see a mum cuddling her kid in a restaurant or you'll feel a surge of love for your own child and ask, 'Why wasn't I good enough?' no matter how many people raise you by telling you none of it was your fault.

It takes a shitload of work to understand that you were never the issue and it didn't matter what you did, you were never going to be enough for them because it was never about you. It was always about the absent parent. A twelve-year-old boy, whose body is going through the biggest emotional and physical changes it will ever see, isn't in a place to understand or accept that. Now is the time for him to test boundaries, make poor choices and feel things so deeply. We just need to be there to pick up the pieces and, even when things are really awful, and when we feel so devastated and panicked by the decisions he's making, we still have to let him know he's loved.

Since the chat, we put some strategies in place.

He meets with the pastoral lead at his school weekly now. She's an independent ear who listens to him, feeds him yummy biscuits and plays boardgames with him. Honestly, she deserves an MBE for the work she's done with my children over the years but I'm also aware there are so many other kids who need her, and sometimes she just can't be available because she has hundreds of children in the school she's trying to rescue. Still, she works wonders; she tells me that some weeks she and Isaac laugh and joke and he has no worries and other weeks his tears are so large because he's sad or overwhelmed about everything and nothing. She tells me his tears make a splash sound when they hit her floor. She has put him on the list for a qualified counsellor to work with him, because she feels he needs it and deep down I know – coming from a really similar situation – that he does.

I threw his phone in the bin because I could tell time and again that the stuff he was watching on social media channels was having a negative impact on his behaviours. Some of the content in the group chats he was in was absolutely stomach-churning and he was just not mature enough or emotionally ready to cope with the things he was repeatedly flooding his brain with.

The rules were really led by Isaac too. I asked, if he was the parent right now, and this was his son, what would he be saying and doing? He was so upset – genuinely gutted at his own behaviour. He was getting into trouble for the most stupid stuff that I imagine, in the grand scheme of things, he realised he didn't even want to be doing. Once he knew his phone was gone it was almost a relief.

The pressure on kids on social media is overwhelming, not to mention the stuff they're seeing and hearing. Often inappropriate and sometimes downright gruesome, horrifying, sick or sexual videos, music lyrics and photos which are readily available. It's so frightening. We allowed him to keep his iPad with only certain apps that he knows have parental controls. We agreed he would train with the football team at school and so far he's been picked for every match to represent his school. He comes home on time every day and on weekends he has a friend to stay at ours so we know his whereabouts.

Since then, he's been a little star. His schooling has improved. I mean, he gets the odd isolation for being the class clown but he loves the isolation teacher so I think a lot of the time he likes to just go hang out with her. I quite like it: she clearly has a soft spot for him and that type of kindness she shows changes the world for any kid. His friendship group now is really lovely. He's really close with his cousin Alfie again, which is lush, and he just feels more like the Isaac we had before he started year seven. He is the Isaac that I think Isaac himself recognises and he feels much safer and happier being that way.

I suppose sometimes we don't realise that the transition from that last year in primary school to secondary is so great. You go from feeling like you are the big fish in a tiny garden pond to swimming into the ocean with a shitload of bigger fish and scary sharks around you.

I think Isaac kind of felt he was going to have to fight for survival. He was doing well at getting a name for himself, but I hope we've shown him that this is not what it's about. Getting a name for yourself for all the wrong reasons only really affects you in the long run. Now he's a year in he's kind of learning it all for himself. We still have bad days, or moments, but they're far fewer in number, they're resolved much quicker and he just seems to get that. He was the only person that lost out in the end and he knows we don't expect him to be perfect. We never expect any of our kids to be perfect because perfect doesn't exist. Expecting kids not to make mistakes or bad decisions can mean they fall so much harder until, sometimes, you can't catch them.

All we ask is that our kids treat other people well, and when they don't they recognise that and make it better, that they're respectful and that they always look out for the ones having a hard time. A smile a day at the kid who doesn't interact with the world, even if they never smile back, can mean so much. And we ask that they just try their best. That doesn't need to look like the best GCSE grades or winning every race at sports day each year, it just needs to look like they don't act like dicks constantly in class, that they don't stop others who want to learn. I reckon they'll all come out OK.

What I have come to realise is school settings don't work for every child. Not every child can excel in an academic setting and it's really rubbish that there aren't other options available. There should be other education settings in which children learn in a physical way rather than sitting at a desk with a pen and paper. I think one day we will get there but, for now, it's about guiding and supporting them as best we can and reminding them, as we do so many times, it's all temporary.

6

WHAT CO-PARENTING LOOKS LIKE
(AND HOW WE GOT THERE)

Edie turned nine a few months ago. In my last book she was a toddler and I wrote about how things had just become amicable between her dad and me after we split. It had been really hideous for the first few years.

It's remained much the same. Edie continues to stay at her dad's between one to three nights a week. She absolutely idolises him and vice versa.

She has a huge friendship group and she loves school. Out of all of our kids, she is probably the most academic. She does her homework each week without any fuss or hassle and at school she has always been really good. She is insane at art and it's something I really try and encourage.

When Covid hit, a lot of her friends got mobile phones. A phone was something I really didn't want her to have but then her dad bought her one for his house and it was a battle I was losing daily. At that time, she was missing her friends and they were all on an app called Houseparty and playing games so I reluctantly agreed.

Edie reminds me a lot of Betsy in her sass and her love of others, especially Wilby. She is obsessed with Wilby to the point it makes my heart hurt. She dotes on him daily and she's not tired of that in almost three years. When we are in public, she is fiercely protective of him and on the rare occasions other children are unkind because of the way he looks or the things he does which are 'different' to them she gets so angry. I constantly remind her a lot of people don't have awareness of ASD. It may seem strange or weird for other children when they see Wilby doing the things he sometimes does, but she doesn't care. She is the first to educate them, and their parents if need be, and it's just beyond lush.

Out of the six children she is the only one who sees the parent regularly they don't live with. She thrives on spending time with him and she misses him when he works away and she doesn't see him. I've known her dad since I was eleven. We went to school together and we were on and off boyfriend and girlfriend. We were always ridiculously close as friends throughout secondary school and I knew that once he started spending time with her after we split up he would be a devoted dad. It wasn't long after she first began spending time with him that she began to love it. She always wanted to see him and she was excited to spend time with him – the same as she gets excited to come home. It's really lovely to have a child who loves spending time freely with both parents, but it was also an alien experience for me.

I had always had to beg Betsy and Tallulah to see their dad. I would get to dread the drop-offs, when they would cling to me and cry or come home really upset with me for making them stay with him for two nights instead of one like I'd promised. I'll be honest, when Edie was tiny I wondered if it would upset me if she would feel more enthusiastic about her own dad, when she wanted to spend time away from me. Now I'm here, it doesn't bother me. It's refreshing to know she has another parent who loves her as hard as I do. They do stuff together all the time, just the two of them; they go swimming, clothes shopping, bike riding, to the caff for breakfast together and she loves it all. She has a whole family at his house who she loves hanging out with and there isn't a part of me that would change that. If anything, it makes me wish the others could have had the same growing up.

I remember when I would go to work with my dad on a Saturday when I was her age and he would tell me so many stories on the way there whilst a Police or Dire Straits album played in the background on the cassette machine. He would make me pass him all the tools to fix a customer's boiler on a cold winter morning or a tap belonging to some old lady whose husband had passed away. I would sit and chat in the homes of his customers, play with their kids or eat their homemade cakes, then we would go for lunch together. Most weeks, he would pick up a hitchhiker on the way back and always drop them where they needed to go rather than near our own home, even if the detour took us an extra hour or two. He would always tell me you learn the most from strangers, and a lot of the time we did. He would chat to whoever he picked up, with a genuine interest about where they were heading and where they had come from. He would encourage people who were struggling in hard times with advice and I imagine now, looking back, because of my dad, when they climbed out of his van, the experience restored their faith in humanity a little.

What I remember most of all on those Saturdays is how amazing it felt to have him all to myself. I would revel in asking him a million questions and studying his face as he sang along to the words of 'Roxanne' and tapped the steering wheel to the rhythm of the music. I remember how special I felt to spend a whole day with him alone. I'm so glad Edie has that. I'm so happy she has a dad who loves her, because that shapes everything in the world for a child.

I just hope this is it for good. I hope we stay on this page until she's an adult, because although she still feels so tiny it seems like five minutes ago Betsy was this age, and she's now just turned into an adult.

I know the next few years with Edie will be challenging at times and testing. More than anything I want us to navigate those years separately but together, being in union whilst supporting Edie the best we can. There will be times I know we will probably disagree with one another. In the past, when we've been up against it, he's good cop and I'm bad, and the three of us laugh about how Edie has him wrapped round her little finger all the time. What I don't want, if we're at loggerheads over a decision or choice, is to let her see that. I don't want her having that option of playing one parent off against the other. I also don't want her to witness us arguing.

It happened once when we had a huge row at my house because she came home sunburnt and I just lost my mind. In hindsight I could have handled it better, but I didn't because I was furious at how burnt she was. When we argued it got heated and nasty – things were said that should never have been said between us and Edie was absolutely devastated. She almost had a panic attack when I came back in the house and kept saying, 'Do you hate each other?' and, 'Are you not friends any more?'

I was so angry – at myself, him and the situation – but I owned it, because it's what we should do. I apologised to him, to Edie and we moved on. I have to remember we have been separated for almost nine years. To have minimal rows like that in all that time is pretty good going.

(I'm pretty sure the stats would be far worse if we had stayed together!)

Still, I will never be that parent that sides with Edie if she doesn't like a decision her dad has made with good intentions and I hope he feels the same. I'm sure he will – ultimately, we've co-parented OK so far. Her elder siblings also have a good influence on her at both houses because they're all close. When things are bad – which I know they will be at times, from experience – we just need to remember it's temporary, it won't last and we *will* get through it.

Things I've learned about parenting over the last five years

I'm thinking of all the changes I've experienced since I was a mum writing my first book. I feel like there are loads mainly, I suppose, because the kids are older and the transitions they've all gone through in the last five years are huge. Back then, I was a way more shouty mum, which on reflection makes me feel pretty shit. Now I'm not so shouty I realise kids aren't any better behaved for having a parent who raises their voice, orders them about or disciplines them in anger.

I often get asked how I avoid losing my shit with my kids – this question comes up especially on Instagram Stories or live shows, when it's utter chaos and the kids are pecking my head or arguing with each other. I try now not to shout when I feel frustrated. I've learned breathing techniques and I have a toolkit to help me through tough days. In this sense, my therapy has been a godsend.

It wasn't until I decided I didn't want to be a shouty mum that I realised how good it felt not to be one. I used to drop my kids at school then drive to work in tears because of the shouting matches we'd had on the journey. I constantly felt shit for telling them off and for the way that it had escalated between us. They'd gone into school raging or upset and I'd driven off to work feeling angry.

I also realised that often I had got frustrated at their frustration. We are so quick to expect a child to hold it together, to put on a brave face. If they have a day where they are in a bad mood or are emotional it feels like our world as parents has ended, especially if we've spent a fortune taking them to a theme park or trying to do something nice for them. But I have so many bad days, when even the sound of someone eating next to me drives me crazy or I want to stay in bed and hide. I'm a grown woman with a shitload of life experience and coping strategies and I still have shit days when I hate the world and everyone in it.

I also suppose that through their various stages I constantly think about where I was at their age and, wherever I had been at every single one of my children's ages from Edie through to Betsy, life felt hard.

During the podcast I mentioned earlier with Josh Connelly, he explained he works with schools, children, teachers and social workers and he constantly fights to ensure young people are included in the conversations and explanations are given to them whenever they are in any type of difficult situation. He is met by adults saying that they are unsure if it's the right thing to do. They don't want to confuse or upset these children by drawing them into adult conversations which may be inappropriate. As he tells them, and he told me, these children have already been put in an adult world, as I was, overnight.

For me, my story was heartbreaking and messy and still no one spoke to me. By not having adult conversations with these kids, they recognise that 'something' is going on, I knew 'something' was going on because I lost my mum at the age of four and I woke up to a dad who was rocking on the lounge floor, clutching his wedding photo. Three weeks later, our next-door neighbour moved in and was sleeping in my mum's bed.

What happens, when no one speaks to these kids, is they make their own stories up in their heads. I made my own story up in my head. And my story was that my mum was coming back for me. I thought that every single night when I went to bed for ten years after she left. Every single night I would fall asleep with my two fingers crossed, begging in my head that tomorrow would be the day she would come back for me. Only she never did, and when my life at home broke down at the age of fifteen because I was deemed unmanageable, when my social worker removed me from my family home, my mum didn't want me to go and live with her.

I still have the report and paperwork to this day. It records that my mum felt I wouldn't get on with her partner and she refused to allow me to move to Louth from Devon to live with her. My older brother couldn't manage me when I lived with him for a short period because my behaviours had escalated so much. And so I went into the foster care system. I look back at those ten years and I am so angry there were no adults to protect me. I'm so fucking angry that not one adult member of my family sat and spoke to me. No one explained anything to me, no one asked how I was, how I truly was. I had to navigate my way through life when it had all turned upside down and inside out and everyone around me who should have been there to love, care and protect me disappeared without any kind of explanation.

I wasn't allowed to feel anything. I was known as moody since I can remember – everyone used to pull me apart because I sulked so much. Now I'm a mum with so many kids who feel so many things and I think my sulking should have been the least of the worries of the adults around me when I was a child. Why the fuck wasn't I screaming and crying? Why wasn't I smashing shit up in rage? Why wasn't I begging someone, anyone, to tell me where my mum had gone and why my dad had moved in a neighbour and her kids into our home? They had fully taken over my family home less than a month after my mum left.

Why wasn't I letting out the physical pain in wails that I could feel stabbing at my throat and heart in the daytimes and at the weekends when both my brothers and my sister were out of the house? The new kids that had moved in were visiting their dad and all I could hear from my parents' bedroom was the most disgusting, confusing noises being made by my dad and new step-mum.

Those experiences led me into the most awful teenage years, where I made some of the worst decisions and choices imaginable. I always encourage my kids to feel things and to ask questions. Ask as many questions as they want, I will answer anything.

Parenting boys

I encourage the boys to show emotion. I don't discipline them when they punch a kitchen cupboard or kick a door because they feel angry at the situation with their mum. I don't tell them to 'man up' when the tears flood in, as I hear so many other parents still say to their sons.

They ask me everything and anything and they always get an honest answer, no matter how shit that makes me feel, when any of them ask me certain things about what went on when they were tiny. No matter how gross some of our conversations have felt, I never want them to lie awake at night wishing they could ask something that feels forbidden or not showing emotion that is absolutely deserved and needed to help them get through.

I was raised not to feel or to question. It was unsafe to do so and even now it presents in my brain as conflict. It genuinely terrifies me to raise certain things with people. I run two companies and employ twelve staff members but because of my childhood, I am unable to be a manager. The thought of running my team and having difficult conversations knocks me sick. This is something Jo and Josh have to do. In the same way, the very thought of having to parent my kids when things are bad and be the parent I know they're gonna hate is the worst feeling. What most people would see as a debate or conversation with a friend, work colleague or partner grows in my brain until it feels like I will explode.

As a result, I ensure my kids feel whatever they want whenever they want. They get emotional and they know that, no matter how bad their choice or decisions have been, if they've hurt someone else with their actions, we can speak about any situation, their thoughts and feelings. We sort it all out together, without any judgement, cross words or feelings of shame and embarrassment.

Turning down the volume

I watch parents through my sunglasses every day when I'm out and about, probably more so since I've had Wilby.

I'm aware I get judged in public. I'm also intrigued by the way other people do stuff. Every single day – if you just sit and look around – you will see parents getting upset and angry with their children for being upset and angry.

Parents physically smack their kids as punishment because they've hit their siblings or another kid on the climbing frame in a park and it wrecks my brain that we still think it's OK. Dishing out threats to our kids whilst we are full of anger is going to make them learn not to feel things that actually are life skills. I don't think I've ever seen a positive outcome from an escalated adult trying to de-escalate an escalated child. It's a life skill to feel a range of emotions and know it's OK to show them all. It's our job to help our kids learn to manage their feelings.

Screaming that something is wrong or disciplining them when we don't like what we see them do, just makes children either angrier or hold onto their feelings and submerge them. This is like creating a ticking timebomb when they get to an age where their bodies change both physically and emotionally from a child into an adult.

Before I opened the women's centre I did some training with the Nelson Trust, a leading charity in the UK whose work and dedication to trauma-informed approaches is absolutely incredible. It was so eye-opening. In 2017 they introduced their 'Becoming Trauma-Informed' responsive guide team who champion their principles. They ensure all their services, staff and volunteers have the tools they need. In 2018, I did a training day with them which was hosted by Dr Stephanie Covington, who came over from the USA to give a presentation on addiction, trauma and recovery. Once you learn how crazy it is to speak to people and treat them the way our society does, you start seeing it everywhere.

Whether parents or teachers towards children, airport staff in security, prison guards or a parent or carer, certain people hold some kind of (what they deem to be) authority. Some think that they can scream and shout, bark orders and address people by their surnames. And for what? To feel powerful or in control? I don't get it. We're all human, no matter what we earn or what our job title is; we all deserve and should expect the same respect and kindness from one another.

Some of it just hurts my heart. To hear that prison officers shout at prisoners, calling them only by their surnames and ordering them around. They have no idea what their background is or what life may have looked like for them. I have met many women who have had custodial sentences. They were never going to walk any path other than the one that led them to a prison cell because they were never protected as a child or teenager by the people who could have made sure things were different for them.

I recently went to Mallorca with our whole family and Betsy's friend, meaning Josh and I had seven children in tow. Wilby being autistic meant it was harder than we envisaged. We got a sunflower badge and special assistance yet we still had to take him through passport control with everyone else. It was genuinely horrendous. All the staff were screaming and shouting and ordering passengers about, getting angry when boxes to stow possessions didn't come down the conveyor belt quick enough. They were all snapping and huffing and puffing, pointing at where things should go, people should be, splitting families into different queues without any explanation to move things along as fast as possible. All the slamming and banging and beeping made *me* feel panicky and it sent Wilby over the edge. He fully lost it.

Yet when we returned via Palma de Mallorca airport we were treated differently. They had a whole separate passport control area for families travelling with special educational needs or disabilities. It was calm, quiet and not brightly lit. The staff spoke in calm tones rather than shouting. It wasn't crowded. And guess what? Wilby didn't lose it. He didn't cry or panic or have a meltdown. He was absolutely fine.

What would be the difference if the prison officers called the prisoners by their first names and spoke to them in a normal tone rather than shouting and ordering them about? What if all the staff at Bristol airport went over to Palma de Mallorca and looked at how they run things, watched how everyone in the Spanish airport security department has managed to chill the fuck out? And be friendly to the passengers? What if they copied what they do and just spoke rather than shouted and they passed the boxes to passengers gently and advised them where to go in the queues in a calm voice? What would the difference be? I feel like, for a start, everyone would have a much better day on both sides – whether you're the person who is dishing out the orders or the ones being ordered. They'd both feel way more positive and happy and actually have a lot fewer feelings of stress, anxiety and depression.

It is just so weird. Why can't we all, as humans, just slow the fuck down and be calmer and kinder to each other? Surely it would make for a much better life on this planet?

In parenting, and to feel like I am the best version of me in society, I often go back and revisit my past. I go back to when I was a child, a teenager, when I was in an abusive relationship and the years after that when I felt so lost. I think, What would I have needed? And, you know, every time the answer is: love and support without judgement. Just those two simple things. Free things that we are all capable of giving to other people.

If every child, every teenager and every adult had just one consistent person to love them and take care of them without judgement the world would be an easier place, but so many don't. It's hard for us to see that, because the majority of people we know do have an abundance of love and support. It's normal to have loads of people around you but always remember that some don't have that. Some children have never felt loved and, just as heartbreakingly, neither have some adults. Some humans have gone through all their childhood transitions to get to the age of an adult and they have never had just one person love them, not one, which is why it's absolutely our jobs to look out for others, to be kind and free of any judgement.

It's just as important to ensure our kids know how to do this; that they have the tools to take care of others – the quiet ones, the disruptive ones and even the ones that at times aren't very nice to others. None of us knows what goes on behind closed doors. This has become more and more obvious as we see the headlines relating to the devastation that can happen when no one saw the signs, no one thought that a particular child would be murdered by their parent or that woman would be beaten to death by her husband.

It's absolutely our responsibility, whether for our kids' friend, a child we teach, a quiet mum in the playground who just doesn't seem 'right', or a neighbour who lives alone. I believe it's our job to ensure that in life, we make sure we are that 'one person' for someone.

7

LOVE AND TROLLS

Christ, I feel like this is going to be a whole book in itself!

I've seen other influencers cover trolling in their books, on their social media platforms and in various articles, but really to date, I don't think any of them have done it justice. I get it, because we don't want to feed trolling, we don't want to draw more attention to it. But the reality of what people like me go through on the internet is absolutely fucking soul-destroying. It's wrong and it's sick and for the first time I feel I should draw attention to it properly. It took over a huge chunk of me and my family, for far too long. Let's start from the very beginning.

I remember writing a little in my last book about the negativity I encountered online. I was told I was a crap mum in a comment on one of the posts I had written. Hundreds of people tore apart my appearance in the comments section of a newspaper article. All this really affected me, until I realised they were doing the same under every newspaper article. There will always be people who don't like or agree with my views or story. I learnt to accept it for what it was and it was manageable. I didn't look at the comments section on newspaper articles again.

I look back at that time, at how it made me feel, knowing I had absolutely no knowledge of what was to come and it makes me feel a little bit sick. Because, within a year of my book being published, I was going to feel a level of hatred I never knew existed.

I wrote earlier in this book that I enjoyed being pregnant with Wilby, and I did, until 31 May 2019, when I was just over six months pregnant and about to board a train to go to King's Lynn to do a book signing. An email pinged into my inbox from a woman. The name on the account didn't meet the sign-off and it was one of the longest emails I had ever received. She claimed to be a journalist who was 'looking into many influencers'. The email started out quite well but it was clear as I read through it, then re-read it, that it was intended to fill me with fear and panic. She was questioning my intentions, everything I had written and told me she was liaising with large tabloid papers to 'look into me and others further'.

I had worked tirelessly with many charities to fundraise. Alongside that we had opened a Paypal account. We used the donations for agencies or women and children themselves, so they could buy new items which they needed when they had left a refuge to go into their own homes. This contact was requesting that I provide evidence of the transactions of the money we had raised as I was being investigated for fraud.

I immediately called my accountant panicking about whether I had done anything wrong and if I should share this information publicly to prove my innocence. It was physically impossible to provide proof. The monies had been sent to named people and organisations and sharing their names publicly would put them at huge risk. I couldn't share details of transactions with names and organisations blanked out because it proved nothing: I could have been sending the money to anyone.

I had taken professional advice when we began our work. I knew that, as long as we had detailed records of everything and we paid everything we should have, which we did, I hadn't done anything wrong. I also knew from the constant feedback from these women, charities and organisations that we had changed the lives of so many families.

The legal advice was to ignore the email, so I did.

Soon after, this woman contacted me again, with two web links. One went to a gossip website and one to a website that she had put up to host an article which did nothing but abuse me.

I clicked on both links and projectile-vomited immediately.

The gossip website was full of comments from people

that held such hatred for me I couldn't comprehend it. Her own website was basically a re-worded version of her letter but edited for the public to read, making all kinds of threats and allegations against me.

Again, I sought legal advice and was told to ignore it, so I did.

The following week Josh and I went on a local hypno-birthing course.

I went on my Instagram Stories in the morning to say I would be in the course until late afternoon and wished everyone a happy Sunday. I came out of the course to find my phone had blown up with notifications. This woman had been on the gossip website and shared her website link to the trolls which led them to the article she had written about me. The other people on the hate website had obviously revelled in it and they all then planned together to target anyone they could with the link to lead as many people as possible to the article. They knew I was going to be away from my phone for the day and unable to manage their comments.

In the six hours I had been in that course they had trolled every part of my life they possibly could. They had all set up numerous fake, nameless, faceless accounts and cut-and-pasted the link to the website under as many of my posts as they could on Facebook and Instagram. They inboxed it to thousands of my followers, posted it on the comments section of huge newspaper articles and alongside viral posts that other influencers had shared and they sent it to every charity and organisation and brand that had ever been associated with me.

My notifications didn't stop sounding and my friends were sending me screenshots of people I passed in the street, friends of theirs, who were sharing the article with their own disgusting opinions. We were driving home from the course and I had a full-blown panic attack. I just couldn't keep up with the notifications and I didn't know how to make it stop.

Josh pulled the car over and tried to calm me down but it was impossible.

He kept reminding me that I was heavily pregnant and I needed to think about the baby but I just couldn't manage to pull myself together. At home, I asked him to leave me in the car for five minutes so I could calm down before the kids saw me. He refused at first but agreed that he would check on me if I didn't come in within a few minutes.

I continued to delve into what was happening, reading more and more comments and posts on Facebook and Instagram and the shares from people . . . so many shares. I was receiving thousands of messages from my followers, sharing the link back to me in case I wasn't aware of what people were saying. I made the mistake of going on the gossip website. The things they'd written about me and the things they'd said about my children were insane. They were also now as excited as a bunch of hyenas fighting over a rotten animal carcass at what they'd achieved in the six hours I was offline.

This 'journalist' behind the article was impressed by her newfound popularity on that site, the hits to her own website and the fact her vile article full of lies and false allegations had been shared far and wide. She decided to come out and reveal her real identity. She had taken to her Instagram Stories publicly, calling me crazy, laughing at me and mocking me for thousands people to watch. A total stranger who I had never spoken to absolutely hated me and she had set out to destroy my life.

I looked at her pages on Instagram, Twitter and Facebook. She was a mum, she was married, she had children – sons. She was raising a little boy a similar age to one of our little boys. My mind was blown that, rather than spend time with him, she had chosen to sit and stalk every part of my life, my past posts and delve into my history. She had contacted members of my family to ask questions about me. She had sent an email to me at such length to cause me, a total stranger, from the other end of the country, in my third trimester of pregnancy, such distress and upset. She must have spent days . . . weeks, doing all of this to me. And when she got no response she did this. For what?

The more I looked into her the more I saw she had called herself a blogger in various posts. She always used blogging chat hashtags which I know many people do to increase their following. Many of her posts were controversial and political and she'd also had an article written about her in a national newspaper.

By this point, every single one of my friends had contacted me to ask what was going on. I knew I had to answer because it was just worsening. I looked like I had something to hide if I didn't respond so I took to my Instagram Stories to explain 'my side'. I named the gossip site where they all congregate to do nothing but rip into people with social media followings.

I look back on that day in hindsight where I recorded those Instagram Stories, at my naivety, at my sheer lack of understanding or knowledge of what was to come once I hit 'post'. I just wish I'd met someone else who had 'been through it' to advise me on how to manage it better.

I took to Facebook and wrote a post explaining what I had said in my Stories. I wrote an open letter to the gossip site begging them to think about the damage they were causing to people's mental health.

I remember calling Laura, who runs her page Knee Deep In Life and just sobbing, and she helped me word the post because I was such a mess. I remember hearing her desperation for me, her 'sorry's because she didn't know how to make it better for me. I just needed someone with a large following who got it but she didn't get it because she'd never been subject to it. She tried with her whole heart to support and help me. She checked in daily and was a tower of strength for me.

And the overall support I received was phenomenal, the love that poured from good people was incredible. But, by retaliating publicly, I also alerted more bitter people full of hate to the gossip website, which encouraged more people to read that article. They formed an opinion of me based on such hideous allegations and lies.

The reality of adult bullying

I remember speaking to my solicitor. She's from Doncaster and I chatted to her originally through Instagram. She carried out some work for me and she is incredibly knowledgeable and a director in her firm.

She looked into everything, and we tracked the 'journalist' (who wasn't a journalist). She found her address and her husband's place of work within hours. She looked into the 'gossip site' that was not a gossip site. It was a hate site.

When I made that website known, thousands of my followers went on to defend me. Every single one of their comments were deleted in seconds and their accounts were shut down. They were unable to create new accounts as they had their IP addresses blocked. If you viewed that website you see influencers with followings far larger than mine. Take Mrs Hinch, for example – she has over four million of the most dedicated followers and she is the leading influencer in the UK. On any of the threads about her there was not one nice or positive comment, and the minute one went up it disappeared within seconds. How would an influencer with over four million followers not have just one positive comment, out of hundreds of thousands of ones full of poison and vitriol? Exactly.

My solicitor pointed out to me that this wasn't a gossip site because the people using it weren't gossiping, they were spreading lies about me and my family and thousands of other mums, dads, daughters and sons. They would take a screenshot of videos of the influencer they hate the most, looking as bad as possible and set it as their profile picture. You know who hates who the most from their profile pictures and they create threads on every single person they hate and they set out to destroy them.

And although, within forty-eight hours of me talking about that site and the awful article, the support I had was incredible, the hate towards me had now quadrupled. There was someone from the school playground reporting on me. One day they wrote about me waddling into the playground in a green dress and sunglasses then tore my appearance apart. They told everyone how hated I was by other mums in the primary school my kids went to. Other people took pictures of me secretly when I was in public and posted them with things like, 'Look at the state of her today.'

Other mums who stood near me in that playground, mums I didn't know and hadn't ever spoken to, had shared the article about me on their Facebook pages. They called me a fraud and a child abuser. The worst part was that local men, those who I had gone to school with, were sharing this article and writing the cruellest things about me. People I classed as my friends told me their Facebook friends were sharing the most awful stuff about me, yet they didn't challenge them, unfriend them, defend me or question it. They remained friends with them. It was like they were just telling me for gossip's sake. But this wasn't gossip, it was my life. It wasn't making any sense.

This continued until the journalist-who-wasn't-a-journalist removed her article, shut down her website and closed down her Instagram account. She remained on Twitter and wrote a few posts which were clear digs at me before she then blocked me altogether.

For the first time in a long time I became poorly. Really poorly, to the point there were days I didn't want to be alive any more. I became so unwell that I cried constantly. I look back at our pictures from when I was heavily pregnant and I see how puffy my eyes were, how physically and mentally unwell I was and it makes my heart hurt that it happened. That had been my happy pregnancy yet turned into probably my worst pregnancy. I wouldn't wish that feeling on anyone.

I remember a night shortly after it all came to light, a whole year after my book had been published. My publishing team got in touch to ask me to take a look at my book reviews. I went on to Amazon and wanted to be sick. Every few minutes another negative review appeared, saying the book was full of lies and I was a fraud. Some didn't even leave a review, they just wrote lengthy, abusive posts about what a disgusting person I was and advised people not to 'buy into me' and encouraged people to join the hate website. My editor managed to contact Amazon and get most removed, but they just kept coming and many are still there today. I logged onto the gossip site and saw it was their latest plan. This is now my life, even today as I write this.

It's also the life of anyone who has any kind of following on a social media platform. We are all targeted by these people in ways you wouldn't even imagine, daily.

I stopped looking at my book reviews, I got my best friend G to manage my Instagram account, uploading content, replying to messages and 'pretending to be me' for a while. Every now and then I would coat my swollen, tear-stained face in concealer and bronzer and take a picture pretending to be the happiest girl in the world whilst Josh whispered, 'Don't let them win, baby.' I would hit the 'post' button whilst my tummy was loaded with butterflies and I just wanted to disappear.

I remember thinking no one understood me. This was a unique situation. When I'd struggled with postnatal depression with the girls I could speak to friends who'd been there or seek specialist support; when I left an abusive relationship my friends and family had witnessed my struggles for ten years and were so supportive. I went into a women's refuge when things got really bad. Nobody could get what was happening now. There was not one other person I could speak to that had this experience – bullying on a scale I'd never seen before. A ton of online hate was pouring on me from every direction.

I felt so hated, so alone. Josh and his mum did all the school runs between them because I couldn't face the playground. Josh's sister and my best friends did everything they could to help but I genuinely have never ever felt so unwell in my life. There would be days that the thought of Josh going to work and leaving me actually made me think about the best way to end my life. I was so frightened about being honest with him because I was aware he'd come from a similar place with the boys' mum and I know what that did to him mentally. I always wanted to be well and happy for him.

I feel so broken now as I type this, remembering that I felt those things. I keep having to take pauses whilst typing because I hate thinking of the pain I was in back then. Strangers on the internet and mums of other children in my playground, men that I went to school with and my daughter's grandmother made me feel like I didn't deserve to live. And in the end, I couldn't hide it from Josh, because

I knew if I told no one the chances are I wouldn't be here much longer. I was looking into ways to take my own life and I would sit there looking at my bump moving, planning when would be the best time to do it. Josh needed to be able to cope the best he could after I gave birth.

I remember the day it all came to a head. The kids were off school for the summer holidays and I hadn't left the house for weeks. Josh was working all day and they were really bored and desperate to go out. I only had Edie and Isaac and so I psyched myself up to take them to China Blue, a pottery painting place in Totnes.

As we were driving along a one-way street in Paignton a car sped towards us the wrong way. There were two lanes of traffic and all the cars ahead started driving up the pavements and beeping their horns, people were screaming out of their windows and pulling into laybys to avoid the car. Edie started crying in panic and it must have been just a millisecond but I remembered thinking if I just stayed still the car would hit me and I would die and it would all be over. When I think about it now, it feels like for ever I was weighing up whether to try and pull over. I mounted the pavement and the car flew past and I got in a total state. I later found out from the news that it was involved in a police chase. I remember that was the point I knew I needed to get help.

I looked at Edie trembling and saying, 'Are you OK, Mummy? Is the baby OK?' And the guilt that consumed me for having 'those thoughts' whilst she was in the car was just devastating.

When Josh came home that day I remember sitting on the edge of the sofa after the kids were in bed trying to explain how I felt but I couldn't get it out. I couldn't explain what I felt and I just kept repeating through heavy sobs, 'My brain is so poorly, Josh.'

And you know what, his brain was poorly too, because it turns out that's what happens when you're watching your heavily pregnant wife getting abused daily on the internet, constantly being sent screenshots of the devastating things they were saying about you, her, your kids and your unborn baby on that hate site, clearing her inbox every hour of every day so she doesn't see the hundreds of messages being sent from fake accounts which were loaded with such hatred and poison, knowing other men in your town had slagged your wife off publicly on their Facebook pages and seeing 'those mums' in the playground that you know were spreading such venom that you were having to take time off from work to do the school run because she couldn't face anyone.

When he broke down I wondered if actually he had it worse than me. I think in many ways he did, because I pictured this happening to him. I imagined how I would cope if I had to somehow try and make it better for him – ensure our unborn child came into the world safely. I wouldn't have done it. I would have literally lost my mind because the pain that I would see him in and the fact I had no power to just make it stop would have been unmanageable.

We were both really poorly; all the dark thoughts I had he was having. All the nights I lay behind him pretending to sleep, he was lying beside me doing the same. Instead of pretending we were OK we just admitted we weren't. It was like we had reverted back to 2014 all over again. Instead of pretending to sleep we lay awake together most nights into the early hours, watching our baby party and, between sobs, we promised each other we'd get through it. We reminded each other we had come through worse than this.

8

OVERCOMING THE HATE

I remember my friend Chloe came over about eight weeks before I had Wilby. Things were really bad and she told me all about her hypnotherapist. We had shared the same therapist for a while – I was still seeing her weekly. She was lovely and I had processed a lot of my past and she listened and offered her views on why I felt like I did, which helped. But I didn't feel like I was any more prepared to cope when something else bad happened to me.

Chloe had felt the same as I did, so she did some research and decided to give hypnotherapy a bash. Chloe is in her twenties, she is ridiculously stunning and she has a good heart. She was writing a business plan to open her own salon and had her life goals and dreams set out. I remember thinking she just had it all, yet here she was, needing weekly therapy for issues no one really knew anything about. She was honest about having them, and publicly catalogued her anxiety and mental health to help other girls like her going through stuff. She was brave and special, and I really loved her. She was refreshing. So I decided to contact her hypnotherapist.

The following week I had a consultation. I cannot tell you how much that hour and a half helped me. Just this stranger, sitting opposite me in her home explaining the science behind our brains and why we feel the things we do and why we behave the way we do. She had an understanding of positive and negative pathways in our brain, our fight-flight-or-freeze instinct, how our brain makes templates, our attachments and relationship styles. So many things – she made them sound so simple to control. It was a case of retraining your brain. It had to be worth a try. I booked Josh an appointment soon after mine and we both had regular, individual therapy sessions.

She told me she would get me to the point that I could easily look at the hate site without any fear or panic and see it for what it was: a forum full of bitter and jealous people whose issues were their own, not mine. The reality was that to them I could have been anyone. It wasn't personal.

Josh and I made the decision to move forward. We didn't ever want to look at that site again. Mainly because of how unwell it had made us. I'd noticed that the one thing the trolls claim to hate on there is the fact 'we influencers' advertise and make money, yet their site was full of pop-up ads. Every hit the owners of the site get increases their traffic so the joke is they make megabucks every time someone clicks to have a nose or writes another vile comment. Josh and I blocked the site in our settings on both of our handsets and Apple devices and swore to each other we would never look at it again. And we haven't.

We continued to have regular therapy and it was insane how quickly we both saw things for what they were. It was not as bad as it had felt for far too long. I can honestly say I owe my life to my therapist. She genuinely saved both Josh and me from a cloud that was so heavy and dark it hurt. We could never see it disappearing.

She spent the first half of our sessions asking us how we were, what had been 'bad' and 'good' that week. She really acknowledged us. She never ever downplayed the bad, no matter how small it seemed. She also praised the good and I felt like she was genuinely happy for our little wins. She would ask questions like, 'So, on a scale of one to ten (one being the worst you could feel and ten being the happiest) how do you feel this week has been?'

I remember at the start never getting above a three. She would say, 'So if next week we aim for you getting to a four what would that feel like?'

I then listed some positive things. Rather than saying, 'I wouldn't cry as soon as I wake up,' I would say, 'I would feel calm and happy when I wake up.'

She would then ask what that would look like to people who saw me. How would my family know I felt better? Again, I would say positive things like, 'I would be smilier and chattier.'

She showed me that it's all about what you say to yourself, what you tell your brain, how you picture yourself. Even if you don't feel that way, if you say it enough you can start to re-train your thoughts, and then changes happen. And I couldn't believe the changes that happened. Within weeks, and just before having Wilby, I started to feel better. I was not so much happy, but at least I didn't want to not be alive as soon as I opened my eyes in the morning. And after that I started to feel better, day by day for the next few months, until some days I would feel happy or find something funny. When I woke the trolls or the hate site wouldn't be the first thing I thought of and I'd feel proud of myself for that. I felt a little bit like me again, the me I was before that email originally hit my inbox in May 2019.

Josh and I went to sleep listening to soundcasts our therapist made for us. We also listened to meditations by a guy called Andy Puddicombe on an app called Headspace. There was something so soothing about his voice and he did these ten-minute talks. If we woke at 3 a.m. and felt wired he would send us back to sleep, especially on bad days.

I ensured I did breathing exercises and the tapping techniques she had set me every day. She gave both of us different coping mechanisms when anything happened that was a 'shock'. She told us it was OK for us to feel the 'shock' – that part was totally normal – but it was how we immediately managed it afterwards that mattered. Currently, we weren't managing and it was making us both so unwell.

We needed to get to the point we would know it was OK to feel the initial shock but then our brains would go back to our positive pathways, reality would kick in and we would be able to cope. For instance, say we got an abusive message, a new call from the authorities in regard to another malicious allegation or an awful book review. I made a playlist of happy upbeat music so when I got a new 'shock' I would instantly begin doing my breathing exercises and hit play on my phone to help me cope. Josh had one of the girls' hairbands on his left wrist. He pinged it every time he got a 'shock'. The idea was that the reaction he got from the hairband stopped his mind focusing on negative thoughts and broke that cycle.

I cry with laughter as I write this now, imagining us both three years ago – him watching me deep breathing and dancing round the kitchen to 702's 'You Don't Know' whilst heavily pregnant and me watching him repeatedly pinging an elastic band on his wrist whilst looking at the ceiling in despair. But you know what? It got us through and thank the fucking lord because it had only just begun.

How the trolls really work

We never hid our therapy from our kids, and I am SO GLAD we didn't.

In the past year since opening the women's centre I've done lots of training about substance abuse and addiction. The research done on what kids think about having therapy and seeking help is devastating. It would be far more acceptable for a teenager that's troubled to say to their friends, 'I'm gonna go score some drugs' than 'I'm going to a therapy session'.

In our house therapy is normal for our children. Through lockdown Josh and I still had our sessions over Zoom so the kids saw it happening weekly. They knew not to disturb us when we were each having our session and we explained how important they were. Seb and Betsy have much more understanding because they are the regular targets of the trolls but Isaac, Lula and Edie have been told that we need regular therapy to make our brains feel OK. Sometimes we just can't manage stuff by ourselves. So it's as normal as Josh having a Zoom call with his sergeant or me with my editor or a brand. They know not to disturb him or me if I'm writing or recording content for work. In our home, there are no secrets and there is absolutely no shame or embarrassment that we both have therapy regularly.

It took ten months after I posted those Instagram Stories and that Facebook post, a shitload of therapy and too many chats with my solicitor to really fathom how trolls work. They're a bit like toddlers: any reaction is a win to them. It doesn't matter if it's positive or negative. Every time I shared an abusive screenshot, tried to be reasonable after a horrific comment on one of my posts or did another Story trying to 'explain myself', the trolling worsened. They hit me harder, quicker and their tricks became dirtier.

We had blocked the hate website on our phones. If we opened a message and accidentally clicked on a link it would be blocked and we couldn't view it. People would often send us screenshots from the site. Some of them came from more trolls, who just wanted us to see the venom being spread about us, others I think were genuinely decent people who had genuinely just accidentally come across the material and were totally disgusted by what these people were saying. The stuff I was seeing was still grim; if anything it had got worse and there were so many more of them. People were saying they were police officers on the site and were making the weirdest assumptions and allegations about us. Some stated Josh was a paedophile who had groomed me to abuse my daughters. (He had been a serving police officer for fifteen years with an exemplary record at this point.) One person stated I had raped her with another male in a car. This apparently happened in 1994, meaning I would have been twelve years old. These allegations quickly disappeared from the thread along with the account of their author once someone began querying dates and ages. They created a 'guess the date' thread, wanting people to say when my eldest (then fifteen-year-old) daughter would get pregnant. They said Edie was a spoilt brat, both the boys were abused because they'd been starved of a relationship with their biological mum and Wilby was overweight and massively 'behind' because he didn't walk until he was sixteen months old.

The screenshots continued to pour in and I'd like to have had the time to ponder how the people behind them were walking the streets and not in a mental health facility or prison for the things they were writing on the internet. I was just too busy fighting the real-life carnage they were causing.

The first incident happened in September 2019. Allegations were sent to the headteacher of the primary school that Isaac, Lula and Edie went to. The head told me he had no concerns – it was an anonymous email, but he had wanted to make me aware. After that we underwent our first proper children's services investigation due to the trolls repeatedly targeting them with anonymous allegations. This is a common occurrence for many influencers now. Only yesterday I saw Ashley James – who has a huge Instagram following – talk about being investigated by a social worker because of relentless, anonymous claims that she neglects her three-year-old son. She is also heavily pregnant with her second child. Watching her talk about what she's going through made me see the trolls have learned nothing in the past three years. If anything they've worsened.

The kids told us they had been taken out of class and they wondered why they had been 'interviewed' about their home life, what went on and how they felt. I wanted to kill. I cannot explain the anger I felt. Josh called their school and spoke to the pastoral team and, whilst they reassured us that they had told children's services they believed the allegations were malicious they said that they had no choice but to remove our kids from their classes. The children had to be spoken to, interrogated – however you want to word it. But they hadn't thought at any point to inform us. They told us it was not down to them. I cried at how fucking wrong it was. Again.

I called both Betsy's and Seb's school. They hadn't yet been spoken to but I was worried they would be and I needed both schools to understand the impact it could have on them. I spoke to Betsy's head of house at her school and heard a different story. She told me she had been contacted by children's services but she point-blank refused to speak to Betsy. She told them that the allegations would not be true and she had absolutely no concerns about Betsy's home life or wellbeing. And I don't know, maybe the rules were different in secondary schools to primary, but surely it should be that all children have to be treated the same? In any case, I literally could have hugged her teacher, for not only believing in us, but also for protecting my baby girl. At that time she was enduring a devastating family court case with her biological dad where she had just been told she may have to give evidence about her little sister. I didn't and couldn't discuss it on my page.

The same went for Seb's school. They just told children's services there was no need for Seb to be spoken to. Still, Josh and I had to sit them down at the dinner table, all five of them, to discuss the trolling.

It turned out Edie, Isaac and Lula had all been asked the same questions at school. One was 'Tell me what frightens you?' Isaac and Lula couldn't think of anything and Edie, who was then only six, said she told them, 'I get frightened when my legs run too fast for my body in the playground and my heart beats quick' and that was it. Three children, their entire worries and only that came up. It made me so emotional.

I asked them all if they'd rather we come off the internet, if they'd rather we didn't do this any more. I could get a job like I used to have but, you know what? They spoke more sense than any adult I had confided in. They were so angry I was even considering deactivating my account because I was being bullied off the internet. They wanted to hold on to what we had. For the first four years Josh and I had been together, I rarely did school runs. I was always rushing to get to work, working in the evenings. They spent winters packing wine glasses and calendars with Josh and me in the evenings just so we got some time together. Nowadays I was available to drop the kids off and pick them up, make their tea and watch films with them. I was present and they wanted that, they loved that. I remember sitting there cuddling Wilby, who was just five months old, whilst trying not to cry and apologising to the three little ones for what they'd been through that day.

Betsy stood up, walked over to me and, as she kissed my forehead, she said, 'Justin Bieber has it worse, Mum.'

We all giggled and I knew she was right. I was allowing people I didn't even know to destroy my livelihood. To take from my baby's future and to stop all the good work we do. Fuck that. Fuck them.

We carried on trying to live our lives but by this point my page was getting busier with campaigns. The trolls must have known this meant I was earning more money and they worsened again. The allegations they made were daily, everywhere. It went from the kids' school and children's services to the police and Action Fraud. They targeted charities I worked with. They hit Action For Children and Women's Aid hard. They contacted Trevi, where I was a patron and Kidscape, where I was an ambassador, and made up so many lies and allegations it was scary.

Anything they said about me I could evidence was untrue and, in fairness, those organisations saw it for what it was. They all continue to support me and work with me to this day. But the trolls discuss this on their hate site. I know, because of the screenshots we have seen over the years. If one of them makes a false allegation they'll tell the rest so they all join in. They also have numerous fake accounts. They make a batch of allegations to the same services or organisations which just increases the volume they're being hit with.

Children's services and charities cannot ignore these malicious allegations. They have a duty of care to investigate. Needless to say, whilst they are looking into my family and that of Ashley James and so many other influencers online, they aren't looking into the families that need it. There are children in the most dire, dangerous situations who social workers aren't getting to because they are spending time and resources investigating innocent families. We only have to look at Star Hobson and so many other devastating cases. These children were not protected, they weren't saved and they were murdered in their homes by the people who were closest to them.

Children's services should have had the time to look at all this. I don't know how these people compiling emails or picking up the phone to call and complain about Josh and me abusing our children don't see that. They don't stop and think about the time and resources they are stealing from the most beautiful vulnerable children who need it, but that's their reality. The people who hide behind a screen in today's world really are dangerous.

After the trolls got no joy with children's services they moved onto the brands that I advertised with. I remember I did one advert with a baby skincare company and the trolls took a screenshot of a video where Josh was cutting Wilby's hair. He had his eyes shut and I filmed him because he was so relaxed but the screengrab made it look like he was squinting. They sent this to the brand and asked why they were working with me when my husband was a child abuser. Every brand I worked with was targeted. Most ignored it but some sent me the screenshots of the messages they had received via Instagram without covering the senders' profiles. Being human, and inquisitive, I often looked up these profiles on Instagram and Facebook. Every single one of them was female and responsible for raising children. Our future generations are being bought up by mothers who, rather than sitting and spending time with them colouring a unicorn book, watching TV together or building Lego, were stalking my Instagram Stories from fake accounts then spending their time – so much time – plotting and planning to destroy me. It's just not something that is comprehensible in my world.

When Betsy got a job at a local ice-cream cafe, I did an Instagram Story in which I made reference to her being such a hard worker as she had done a long shift. I accidentally showed her work badge in the video. Two hours later, I was in bed asleep when Betsy woke me up, saying her manager was trying to speak to me. She had a baby who was just a few weeks old and was on maternity leave. She told me that her business Instagram and Facebook pages had been targeted with messages from various accounts with zero followers or posts, stating that she was illegally employing a minor and they were going to have her investigated. She was in a total state.

I told her not to panic. I tried to explain a bit of the background story but, as I said earlier, people who haven't experienced it just don't get it, and why would they? I could tell she was still so worried even when I told her nothing would come of it. They were trying to inject panic into her because they had nothing better to do.

The next morning she called me to say Torbay council environmental health department had been informed of illegal working practices using children and they wanted to do a full investigation into her business. I felt the 'shock'. I played my music and did my deep-breathing but that day I projectile-vomited and felt such guilt at what I felt I had caused. The environmental health inspector visited and did say that Betsy's employment was in fact illegal because she didn't have a permit. She had one for her previous job but apparently she needed one every time she got a new post.

I called the inspector and explained the situation. Due to Covid the council offices had only a skeleton staff and they weren't issuing permits. Betsy wasn't allowed to have a job and the other fifteen-year-olds who worked there had now also been let go with immediate effect. I instantly lost it.

I pulled the car over to take the phone off handsfree. I sat outside a fish-and-chip shop in Preston where they were queuing out the door to order their takeaway and I just cried down the phone at the officer in sheer frustration and despair in front of everyone. I knew these anonymous emails weren't about protecting kids who were working a few hours a week in a nice environment under a good management team.

This was malicious. It would have been hatched as a plan on the hate site to get my daughter sacked and upset an entire business in the hope people would turn on me, nothing more than that. These kids could have been out hanging round the streets smoking weed, drinking alcohol and getting up to no good. Instead, they were spending their days working, which in turn taught them values and set them up for life. The guilt that swept over me that one day, that a load of fifteen-year-olds had lost their jobs because of one Instagram Story by me was unbearable.

I had to sit Betsy down and explain that she could no longer work because they'd reported her in such high volume, as they always do. I know now that one person will have a multitude of fake accounts. They just keep hitting send on their messages to authorities and make calls from withheld numbers. Of course, none of that mattered to her. She just sat there, totally confused and disheartened and said, 'I just don't get it. When I don't work they send me messages from fake accounts calling me a spoilt little bitch and when I do work they get me sacked anyway. I can't win, Mum.'

I apologised through tears. All I wanted to do again was take to my Instagram Stories and scream, 'Are you fucking happy now you've destroyed my baby and all her friends? Are you happy you've upset a woman trying to run a business with a tiny, newborn baby? Are you fucking happy, you evil bastards?' But I didn't.

Instead I emailed Sara and asked for an emergency therapy session. No matter how much I danced round the kitchen, breathed in and out and tapped my fucking forehead, I could feel my brain getting that poorly buzz. I couldn't shift the negative thoughts and I felt really frightened. A few hours later, after an intense, extra-long therapy session, I was back to being me and telling my brain, 'We can win and we will – we will fucking win.' I started planning how to get there.

9

TURNING THE TIDE

I didn't leave the environmental officer alone.

She was actually genuinely really lovely and supportive but I imagine by the end of that week she was more sick of hearing from me than the constant anonymous allegations she was receiving daily. It took three weeks and a huge battle, but Betsy and the others had their jobs reinstated, legally, with the permits they needed.

The following week I missed a withheld call, then got the usual text message asking me to call a social worker back urgently on a local number. My belly flipped but I reminded myself what Sara had taught me: 'The shock is OK.' It's how you go on to cope after that which counts. Josh was at the gym and I was with all the kids, in the throes of home schooling.

I called her back and she was the most confrontational, unsupportive social worker I have ever dealt with. I knew instantly I had my work cut out. She told me she needed to see the children as she'd received anonymous complaints that I was physically abusing Seb and I was an alcoholic. I explained I had a baby under the age of one I was breast-feeding and I wasn't drinking any alcohol. I also advised her to look at our notes on the system but she wasn't giving up. She asked me to put Seb on the phone so she could check he was OK.

My brain hurt at that request. How can you check the welfare of a teenage boy with a phone call where he's stood next to the woman who's supposed to be abusing him? I could be making hand-gesture threats or I could have muted the phone and warned him about what to say to her. In any case, the reality was, passing him the phone with no explanation other than, 'This is a social worker who wants to ask you some questions' would have sent his anxiety through the roof. The panic he would have felt would have made him sound like he was being abused. I refused and said she would need to call Josh for authorisa-tion. I ended the call and I breathed in and out and danced round the kitchen to my faithful, old-school R&B tunes. The kids didn't bat an eyelid. It was quite a normal sight by this point to see me open something on my phone then start deep-breathing and finger-dancing round the kitchen to Beyoncé for five minutes.

I told Josh and he was absolutely livid. He came home and rang the social worker from the front drive so the kids couldn't hear. At times like this, I would pay to have Josh's resilience and assertiveness. He has the ability to manage a situation calmly, injecting facts and reality and he also has the power to serve someone their own arsehole on a plate at the same time. He makes them aware of how badly they've fucked up.

As he spoke to her, he paced up and down the drive. He fired questions that she simply couldn't answer. The most important point, the one that destroyed their whole case, was that they had sought the children's medical records, spoken to all their schools, interviewed three of the kids, retrieved family court documents and repeatedly harassed us yet no one had been out to do a welfare check on our baby. He was the most vulnerable out of all of them. He hadn't been seen by a doctor, midwife or health visitor since he was a few weeks old. The only hospital admission he'd ever had was when he had accidentally eaten part of a firelighter he managed to get out of a box in the lounge. I panicked and rushed him to A&E and he wasn't in a nursery setting. He never left the home without Josh or me, so surely he was at huge risk?

The social worker told Josh that couldn't be true, he repeated it was and she checked the system and apologised, saying it was something she would look into immediately. Josh then went on to ask what their protocol was. Sometimes we were investigated by them, sometimes we weren't. I remember the way his questions just kept coming, relentless. He was saying, 'How many anony-mous reports do you get before you investigate us? Because this is never going to stop; so what is it – five? Fifteen? Fifty? How many?'

She couldn't give him an answer. She said there was 'no set number'. He then went on to ask who would give us protection as a family from these people on the internet who were taking vital resources away from the children who desperately needed their intervention.

I remember him being angry but I could also see him working hard to stop his emotion pouring out. He was saying, 'Where is the protection for my sons not being ripped out of their class and spoken to after what they endured during family court for so many years; and, in 2016, after speaking to every service and profession going I promised them it was finally over? I promised them that never again would they be interviewed as children by a person in authority about their childhood again? Where is my wife's protection, that she won't be constantly receiv-ing these calls for nothing else than having an online pres-ence that makes strangers on the internet bitter and jealous?'

The social worker's end of the phone fell silent.

Josh told her that we did not give permission for them to contact our children's schools, speak to them or arrive at our home unannounced. He said, 'Go have all the meetings you want about our kids but know that none of them are with our consent or permission and before you ever turn up here ensure you have a warrant or a court order with you.' He wished her well and ended the call.

When social workers had first been involved, I had naively written an open letter across my channels begging the trolls to stop. I said children who were actually being abused and neglected were at further risk because social workers who should have been spending time with them were with us. I soon learned I had just kicked the hornets' nest. They rejoiced that they had got a reaction and continued to make more anonymous complaints.

That day, I sat on the top step of our house and sobbed into Josh's shoulder, upset and in sheer rage at these fuckers, whilst he was shaking with anger. He kept repeating, 'Remember, we just have to get comfortable with being uncomfortable.' And we also had to not react, because that's all they wanted. Fuck giving them a reaction, no matter how much I felt like I was going to explode.

For so long I wondered what 'they' looked like. I was genuinely curious about their appearances, whether they had jobs and if so which ones. Did they have children or a partner? The more their hatred grew the sloppier they became and I now know what so many of them look like in real life. Sometimes they fire off an abusive comment under one of my posts from their genuine account. They quickly delete it before posting pretty much the same from their fake account because they think I'm 'too busy' to have spotted it. They don't get a reaction from me and they take their chances again. They also often message brands to make complaints about me from their real social media accounts so it looks more legitimate and often those brands just send them onto my email so I often see their usernames.

I wonder how it will work out for them when they spend so much time behind a keyboard writing thousands of posts on a hate website and interacting with other like-minded people. They all spend their time stalking people, obsessing over what they do. They then work out the best ways to target us. They spend more of their time emailing brands, trolling book reviews, contacting various services. They send Betsy or Seb horrific messages, they contact the police to say I am a domestic abuser; it is relentless. They stalk and harass every single part of my life and if you tracked them down they'd either justify it or absolutely shit a brick. Most would justify it in their own heads and to each other in their grim little corner of the internet.

It's the same when a suicide bomber tells himself it's OK to kill innocent people. Once upon a time he too was 'curious' and he went to that ISIS group and met other people who soon normalised their beliefs. All of a sudden something he once questioned became so right that he strapped a vest to his body and murdered innocent men, women and children. Similarly, these women visit a hate site – maybe because they didn't like someone, maybe just to lurk, maybe they came across it by accident or maybe they went on to defend their favourite influencer but came across another one who irritated them slightly. After a while, reading the poison everyone spouts daily, the blatant lies they tell and the venom they spread, it becomes normal and acceptable. They join in and they're met with loads of likes and comments from other people.

Before long they email a brand or complain to social services, because it's justified in their own minds, they encourage one another and they praise each other. It's a really sick, dark part of the internet, but the fact is it's filled with normal-looking women. They are the ones who serve you at the bank, invite your daughter to their house for dinner after school, care for your son in hospital when he has a broken arm or offer to run an errand to help you out if you feel unwell. But their hate pages ruin lives. People who are being trolled have spoken out time and time again, revealing that they feel suicidal. The trolls don't stop – they are literally killing people and they are just relentless.

I have recently come across an Instagram page that hunts and outs the trolls on the hate site. Sometimes the trolls upload screenshots and accidentally leave their Instagram profile picture on the page. This person then tracks the account by the profile picture, links names and what they say. It must be time-consuming but I suppose people are now so sick of it they don't care. She just tracked down one of my trolls.

Another troll, who was outed for writing about a well-known influencer, continued to say, 'I am a nurse' during her tirades of abuse on the hate site. A lot of the time these trolls like to roleplay and make out they're all kinds of weird and wonderful things. I think this is designed to steer us away from their real-life identities. A lot of the time you take what they say with a pinch of salt! But it turns out, this troll was actually a children's nurse, who had an article written about her online at the hospital she worked at, with her picture attached. She looks like she's in her mid- to late-fifties and she has a huge beaming smile in her scrubs. You can see her name badge and the hospital she works at.

She may have been caring for people's children yet she's also sat on a hate site behind a fake account, spouting the most horrific things about innocent human beings, total strangers on the internet. The person behind the page that outs trolls made an entire Instagram highlight. She had taken all her evidence to the hospital the nurse works at. She then screenshotted the nurse's real social media pages, her fake ones and the links she had made and the reams of venom she spat online. She shared the reply she got back from the hospital, showing they were investigating the nurse in question. They reassured the complainant that they have a zero-tolerance policy on bullying. Just like that the nurse disappeared.

The troll hunter sent me the details of my troll over a month ago. My troll had followed my Instagram but her

Facebook account was, unfortunately for her, public. Her employer was listed and her pictures were open and I could see all her friends and family members liking them. I didn't act, I just sat and watched her. My friends kept taking screenshots of the venom she spouted. We sent it to my solicitor. Yesterday I called her out on my page. I hid her name and photo but shared parts of her profile. She is an accounts manager from Norfolk, a married mum of three. On the face of it, her social media platform makes her looks very happy with a nice life (although we know how easy it is to create something that isn't real on social media). She messaged me, at first saying I was wrong. When I told her about all the evidence I had, she replied, 'For what it's worth I'm sorry.'

For months she had been writing the most awful stuff about my appearance, my kids and the type of person I am. It's been relentless. And she wouldn't have stopped, she probably won't stop. She's addicted to spending her time on a hate site talking about a total stranger from hundreds of miles away. Her sorry to me then became, 'I feel sick.' She asked what I was planning to do with the information. If she lost her job her family wouldn't be able to survive without her wage. She wrote, 'I don't know what to do.' She wanted me to tell her what she should do because of her own actions.

I just showed her the things I know she said. That reality has hit her because she said all those things from behind a fake account, where she was anonymous, and now she wasn't. Instead, the person she had written these things about was now in her inbox, asking her why she hated her so much.

I kept asking her what I had done to prompt her to write hundreds of messages over such a long period of time. She ripped apart my appearance, my parenting and she stalked me on Companies House to work out my earnings. She looked into the building construction of my loft space. She was literally one of my worst trolls and I just couldn't get my head around the fact this wasn't personal. This isn't someone I did something wrong to when I was young or who I pissed off at school. A total stranger 249 miles away from me. Five hours up the motorway.

A mum, a wife and a decent career and she chose to sit on the internet and stalk me. And after I wouldn't prom- ise not to contact her employer she blocked me. Then she disappeared, just like the nurse. She was another one – and I don't know what happened to the nurse. I imag- ine that what we can't see is her entire life has fallen apart, because she got so comfortable with abusing people online. She felt the other trolls were her friends, so she spoke openly and honestly about her career. It became so normal for her that she wrote the most disgusting things about mums and dads and their chil- dren. I expect she's then been called into a meeting at work where she will have had to sit in front of her colleagues and, I imagine, people of the most senior level and explain her actions.

Only then, in the cold light of day, does it become so real. None of what you've been doing is normal, right or OK. In fact, it's absolutely soul-destroying. I often wonder, what did she do then? How would she have explained that to her husband and kids when she got home? I can't imagine they knew she's spent the whole of lockdown destroying the lives of influencers online – one in particular that she appeared to be absolutely obsessed with.

And it splits me, because I half feel some sort of relief and hope that these fuckers are now getting caught. When the rest of them see what happens it will send ripples of anxiety through them. They could be the next one. Then half of me still, annoyingly, feels sad that they've fucked their entire lives up, because I don't see how that nurse could ever have kept her job. She's no doubt lost her career, which in turn will have huge implications for the lives of her and her family. How shit for them. It's beyond fucked up.

And there is nothing that justifies their behaviour. There is not one reason they could ever give that could warrant the things they have done to my family. I don't care what they say. These women behave this way because they are jealous of me, they hate my success and they hate that people love and support me. Their hatred is absolutely nothing to do with me. If they were happy within themselves I would have absolutely no effect on them. If they didn't like my content or thought I was a bit of a wanker they'd just unfollow me and move on, like thousands of people do, but they don't, they can't – because they are so unhappy with their own lives that they become obsessed with mine. They stalk every single thing about me and my family. When I block them they set up more fake accounts and somehow they convince themselves this is the behaviour of a normal, happy person.

And so it continues.

Most days we continue to receive abusive messages and most weeks we face a fresh allegation of some kind. Just this month alone they've contacted our local building inspector to tell him we have done illegal building work at our house. They contacted the police numerous times to allege that Josh broke Covid laws last year. Josh's sergeant was told Josh is a victim of domestic abuse and that I physically assault him. They carried out a welfare check at the station.

The trolls continue to contact every brand I work with to tell them a variety of lies about me being abusive and a fraud. I know by the time you're sat reading this chapter that the negative book reviews will have already flooded in, as they always do. On the release of my last book, they all plotted and planned beforehand. When I woke on publication day I was met with the most hideous reviews on Amazon. They had all stayed up writing them once the book was released at midnight.

I arranged an emergency meeting with my publishers and literary agent as soon as I got back from the school run at 9 a.m. As we got on Zoom I could feel the tears coming because I only had negative reviews. I was terrified my publishing team would be disappointed and wouldn't want to work with me again but, instead, they assured me it was actually a good thing, and something they were expecting. It's something they now see so often with so many of their authors. But you see, it doesn't matter if your reviews are good or bad. When you get a huge surge of reviews on a book it helps it get seen. It slides into various Amazon charts and gets into the movers and shakers section. All of these things are massively helpful, so weirdly I was grateful for their hate. They helped me become more successful without even knowing that was what they were doing. I am now a double-*Sunday Times* bestseller and you're reading my third published book! I kinda hope they've already left their negative reviews before reading this paragraph. Some will have, I'm sure. They can't help themselves, so cheers to them!

Choosing strength over hate

The trolls basically, as you can see, do all sorts. Only they've fucked themselves over time because, as Mrs Hinch wrote in her book, this is something we all endure.

The 'rise of the influencer' has sent people crazy. Brands now expect malicious allegations. In fact, if they don't get trolls contacting them they often find it strange. Every person I speak to with a large following is subjected to this kind of treatment.

I hear, 'Why don't you just come off the internet?' from people. But why should I leave? This is my place of work. I have done nothing to have to shut my account down and disappear just to keep people that hate me happy. If an employee at a supermarket was being targeted as much as me, I can guarantee the police would intervene. That supermarket would have an HR plan in place to protect that employee. They would be supported and the person doing the harassing, stalking and abusing would be reprimanded. That isn't there for me.

My solicitor assures me what we can do is take the hate website to court, we can apply to get IP addresses to take the users off that site to court. We could track users who write hundreds and thousands of abusive, horrid, false and disgusting comments about me, my husband and our children. But for now, it's not something I want to do because what's to say another hate website won't start once that one shuts down? What's to say a load more trolls won't appear once this bundle go away?

It's also ended up being a bit of an experiment. I want to see how my Patreon page works with trolling, because people have to use a form of identification to join. I don't get trolled, as a result. They do not risk their identities being outed so they stay silent. Imagine if you had to join all social media with identification. You could still have a private username to protect survivors or anyone else who needs it, but it would mean the trolls' real ID would be logged somewhere.

Social media giants need to step up their game. Anything with the word 'Covid' gets instantly flagged and sends you to a help site yet, if I share something one of my trolls has sent, I will have that content removed and get a warning that I have broken community guidelines with bullying and harassment. It sends me crazy. I am showing where I am being targeted yet no one is held accountable for that.

I did see very recently that Jeremy Vine has been in court in the case of an online troll who targeted him. The troll was imprisoned for five years. It made me feel a sense of relief, and I know things will change. Lives are being lost due to the anonymity people have online and it's wrong. I do believe we will catch up, it just takes time. I hope in years from now it won't be how it is at the moment. People are tired of anonymous online hate. It's not cool or trendy. It's grim and it's becoming apparent that the issues lie with the people writing it, not the ones they're writing about.

For now my therapy helps me manage the 'instant shocks' and the feelings afterwards. All the charities I work with support me and check in regularly. The brands I work with are a hundred per cent behind me and, to date, children's services have closed far more cases than they've ever investigated and I know, as do they, the ones they investigate come to nothing. I suppose as well the saying that you 'grow thicker skin' has become real for Josh and me. Stuff that would destroy other people we now don't bat an eyelid at because I suppose we've normalised it. That's not OK, because we should never have had to, but it's the only thing we can do to keep us here and that allows us to cope.

Things that in 2019 made me mentally unwell I now don't think twice about because I know it won't stop. I suppose I've seen it comes to nothing. If you aren't actually doing anything wrong and you have a kind heart, these faceless, nameless people on the internet are actually powerless. They're everywhere, targeting people like me – and people now just expect them to be there. They know they make up the most ridiculous lies and write the cruellest of things and that's just what you have to remind yourself of on the bad days.

I have six amazing kids and a rock of a husband who are my biggest fans. I have the smallest but most fiercely loyal group of real-life friends. I know the best bunch of influencers. We all flit in and out of each other's DMs, reminding each other we're doing 'OK' and showing one another love and support on difficult days. I also have you and I never take that for granted. You, here, reading this right now.

You've bought my book, you like and comment on my posts, you send me messages sharing your stories or send me love on the shit days and that's why I'm still here, because the good always outweighs the bad, no matter how it feels at times, so thank you. I am forever grateful to all of you!

10

FRIENDSHIPS

I get asked about my friendships all the time, via the comments sections of my posts or my inbox.

I have the most incredible husband and fabulous kids but I cannot stress the importance of having a few true female friends by your side. I am so lucky I have kept friends from primary school. Jo is now the managing director of my company and she was my best friend when we were just five. We were inseparable throughout school. Hannah became my best friend when we were teenagers. I was struggling just to live whilst I was in a bedsit, managing money and trying to be an adult at the age of sixteen. She lost her dad to motor neurone disease and had to learn to live with a broken heart. I'm so proud of how we overcame some pretty shit choices we made together and individually. We remain together today, encouraging and being there for each other when things are shit (I also got to marry her brother, which was always a life goal!).

I also now have best friends I have met on the internet or at my book tours. I truly believe some people are just meant to come into your life from the most weird and wonderful places and they leave a mark which is so beautiful it will never be erased.

For example, one day shortly after I had Wilby I got a message on Instagram. The username was 'astridiwant-youinmylife'. She said she had recently moved to the area from Surrey with her husband. She had found me on insta and wondered if I fancied a coffee as she didn't know many people. I read that message at what was a really bad time because of the online trolling. I wasn't leaving the house because of my anxiety. Whilst Josh was at work I was drowning in loneliness with a newborn so I invited her over to mine for a cuppa.

She rocked up looking so glam and she had bought her own teabag with her to make peppermint tea! She snuggled Wilby and told me all about her life. She was sixteen years older than me. She and her husband had been together over twenty years. He had recently retired from the Met as a sergeant doing the same role as Josh. Talking with her just felt refreshing and unusual. Astrid lives in her own bubble, as I've come to realise, where she sees good things and kind people and she just floats about looking glam as fuck. She's smiley and kind and she's an incredible cook and she's become one of my good friends. She also has a past: she too made mistakes and memories. She doesn't really talk about it online, but she does with me and it feels good.

I realised it wasn't often I made friends with women I didn't need to help fix. We met her husband, Simon. He and Josh became friends and the four of us hung out loads, went away together and did lush stuff for each other. In Astrid I'd made a friend who didn't need anything from me. I had so many people around me who needed me – be it emotionally, physically or financially. Some build an Instagram profile off my following. My friends had become so dependent on me that actually it didn't feel like they were my friends any more.

Astrid and Simon actually did stuff for me. It's true that lots of my friends do this – some of my very best friends constantly think of me and do cute little things for me. On the whole, though, I realised that many of my friendships had changed since I was deemed 'successful'. Now it is actually about what people could get from me.

With Astrid I have an easy, low-maintenance friendship. She would make us lunch, offer to have Wilby when he was tiny or leave a homemade, sticky toffee sponge on the doorstep when she was passing. Simon found Betsy's first car and went to the other side of Devon to test drive it for us because Josh and I had no clue what we were looking at. He often calls Josh to go for a coffee or just check in. At first I thought it was an age thing – they are in their fifties and have moved down here to just chill. But I realised I also have people in my family who are even older than that and are loaded with hate because they deem me successful.

And I have so many friends now who leave me feeling like Simon and Astrid, too many to mention. But this friendship came at a time when some negative stuff was happening and it made me evaluate what I wanted, what I had. I also saw that I had to start getting a handle on the people who weren't like them. It's taken some time but in the past three years I have had to start being aware of people around me and why they are actually there. Now I feel like my boundaries are in place, because I'm no longer here to be the person I've been my entire life. I won't have people treat me the way they have far too often.

Learning to let people go

I won't lie. I feel like the last five years have been the happiest of my life. At the same time, they have without doubt been the hardest and most heartbreaking when it comes to things that have happened with people I classed as friends and family members outside the home.

One of my first friendships ended in 2019 and I felt like I'd been stabbed in the back. My therapist said the friends I pick have a huge impact on why things end up going the way they do.

I'm broken, delightfully broken, as my friend Ben says.

I seem to attract other women who are broken, partly, I think, because I relate to them more than people who have had an incredible childhood and have their lives together. It's also partly because there's something in me that knows you can overcome your struggles and smash life, because I have. Perhaps I want to help them get there.

The thing about having friends who are broken is that a lot of them aren't ready to work on themselves, to address their issues or take responsibility for their actions. A lot live in such denial they don't even see the devastating consequences their decisions are having on them, their lives and the people around them. The choices they make affect me and Josh. Josh has a career in which he can't fuck about and he doesn't want to. Even whilst he is on a career break he is still under full police regulations. Being around my friends who do shit things or keep company with certain people can cost him his job. It is just a simple no. It's something they know they've signed up for.

With me being online, the trolls are obsessed with finding out every bit of information they can about anyone associated with me. I now need to live my life just like Josh does as a police officer. Cancel culture on the internet is a real thing – we see constantly how people who make their living off the internet disappear in a flash once someone digs up old tweets, videos or texts. I cannot hang out with people who are making really poor decisions or are in relationships with people who can cost my husband and me our careers. Ultimately, it's my kids' future at stake.

I do support my friends who want to change. In 2021, I gave evidence in the witness box at crown court in a trial of one of my best friends. At that time I believed they wanted to change. I've spent thousands on rent, deposits and furniture to give friends their forever homes when they are in dire situations. Yet I can't help people anymore who don't want to help themselves.

I can't remain friends with women who can destroy my family with their decisions and some of the time they don't even see that's what they're doing. I don't have the power to change the situation, to help them to change it. For them, there is either no issue or, worse still, they see the issue is me because they feel I should support them no matter what.

That means I have to make some really heart-wrenching decisions. I have strong boundaries, which is something I have had to work really hard on since 2019. I am under the microscope when the trolls spot stuff and come for me. I have to remain silent and dignified, even when things are written and said about me that are the opposite of what has actually gone on.

I had to realise no one came along and saved me when I was a child, a teenager or when I became an adult. It was me that had to make that choice for my daughters' futures. I walked out that front door in 2010 with my two babies and minimal belongings and I worked day and night over years to rebuild myself. I had to work my way up from the trenches to get to where I have today. There isn't one person responsible for that other than me. And as much as I don't want any of my friends to ever struggle like I did, I've come to realise I wasn't put on this planet to just save other people. I've learned from how I've been treated that I cannot just see the good in everyone and I don't have that desperate need to be liked or loved now. I am not a rescuer. I will facilitate supporting people who are saving themselves but I will not do it for them.

The only person who gets hurt is me, over and over again. These are broken people. They are unhappy people. They are people who have no awareness they need to work on themselves. I'm OK with being hated by them. I'm OK with people who cannot cope with me because of whatever reason they give. I don't even need or want to hear their reasons. It's fine and I'm fine. It's a 'them' problem, not a 'me' problem.

Celebrating myself

I've spent the majority of my life feeling ashamed, embarrassed and praying some things I've done never 'come out'. It's only a recent thing that, actually, I feel really proud of myself at times. I recognise the things I endured as a child were not OK. Those things weren't my fault. Yes,

I made some really awful choices along the way from my teenage years onwards, but without guidance and love I think I came out OK. Today I feel proud, I know that I have done incredibly well getting myself out of such a dire situation and achieving what I have. Despite all that I'm still broken. There are still days that the things I did in my past haunt me. There are mornings I sit on my bed and heave with sobs at how angry I am: at my childhood and the things people did and said. I'm angry at how I treated certain people and wonder if I would have done things differently if I'd had a role model.

It's constant, hard work to manage my mental health, my busy brain and to stay focused to achieve my goals. I remind myself I am worthy of them, and of what I have right now.

I remember meeting Josh and, despite the world crumbling around us we were still so happy when we got together. This was despite the actions of others, which I wrote about in my first book. Despite what felt like us battling the world, we were battling it together and we were so in love whilst we were doing it. I suppose for the first time ever my family saw I was loved and supported. Josh loved me so much – and he took care of me. He wanted the best for me, so for the first time in my life I was settled, secure and happy. Part-Time Working Mummy followed and with that all some people around me seemed to see was success.

I never saw the success. Until recently I've massively struggled to be proud of my success. Those first few years, after having built that huge following, I worried it would all disappear or go wrong. I have always lived with this shame, a shadow of the things I have done in my past, mostly when I was young. Much of it I blanked out but so much of it is still there, like a little devil who sits on my shoulder and, when I'm smashing my goals, he whispers in my ear to bring me back down to panic mode.

Last Christmas I got invited to a day out with colleagues I worked with from my teenage years until 2018. The thought of going was too much. I tried to explain it to one of my old colleagues, Kate, but I couldn't find my words. I was just upset at the thought of having to go and see everyone. When we broke it down I realised I'm embarrassed and ashamed of who I was when I worked there. For the last four years before I left the company I was in a relationship with Josh and I was happy and stable. But I'd worked there for well over a decade before then and those years were so ugly at times, they taint everything in my memory.

There were things those people saw that make me so embarrassed and ashamed today. I was so frightened that the only Rach they know is 'that Rach' and I'm not that Rach anymore. I don't want to be associated with her. She feels like a stranger to me. When I look back at her it's like I'm looking at someone else's life. I just want to push forward and forget that part of my life ever existed. It's the same when I see someone from my past in a supermarket or in the street. Once upon a time I would have been in a drug den with that person or doing something else just as grim. That gut punch I feel is a flashback of my old life, the way I lived to survive. It takes so much for me to not feel that shame and embarrassment when I think back to those times, even though I know it wasn't my fault. I was being led by older people and I didn't have a parent to step in and take care of me. At the age of sixteen I was in a bedsit alone. So now, at the age of forty, I work hard to force my brain to believe I did well. I came out OK and I try so hard not to feel that shame.

No such thing as the perfect family

I'm always asked about my family – my parents and my siblings.

I think when you come from a family that's a bit fucked, it feels exceptionally shit because everyone knows someone that has that 'perfect family'. The ones that holiday together every year. All the siblings are really close, they all accept and love each other's partners. They raise their kids alongside one another and spend Christmas together. In the afternoon they eat the most incredible food in a beautiful home before they sit in front of the fire playing cards, having nibbles. All the kids are well-behaved and grateful for their gifts.

Personally, I don't believe there is such a thing as a perfect family. Maybe because of where I've come from, maybe because of what I've spent almost two decades raising or maybe it's the work I do. Maybe it's all of these things combined but to me everything takes work, responsibility, forgiveness and patience, even within the families that look like they have it all together.

Social media has a way of showing all the perfect bits of everyone else. When you have issues within your own family or relationships it makes you feel even worse, or at fault.

After my mum left our family home in 1987, I imagine the feeling being similar to finding out you have an illness but you're not quite sure what it entails. The four of us, her children, were at such different ages. I was four, my brother was nine, my sister was fourteen and my eldest brother was eighteen. We each had to cope with the realisation that our amazing, devoted mum left the family home and, within a short time, moved a seven-hour drive away. She didn't return for twenty years. I don't think any age would have been easier to deal with that. I think we all struggled in our own individual ways, but never together.

It's almost as if we also separated from one another when she left. Yes, I would see one of them, maybe two at a time but I have no memories of the four of us spending time together after she left – either to grieve or have fun. It was like that illness we got then became terminal. It killed our lives as we knew them and we each had to restart alone.

I suppose we plodded on for many years, but because of where we had come from we were all so different. We have all dealt with our childhoods in totally different ways and that has probably driven us apart somewhat too. My eldest brother and sister spent nearly all their childhood being raised by Mum, my brother almost made a decade, but I didn't even make five years. We had the same birth parents, but the way we were raised was totally different. Soon after my mum left, my eldest brother and sister moved out of our family home. From a really young age I didn't see my sister and I only saw my brother on a Sunday when he would take me out for the day. It was tinged with such sadness because I missed him so much that whole day made my heart heavy. I didn't want him to take me home and leave me without him for another week.

I haven't spoken to my sister for over five years and haven't been in contact with my brother since 2020. My mum said, 'I hope your kids never do to you what you've all done to me because it's heartbreaking seeing you all falling out.' And I get that it's shit for her because she speaks to all of us but I had to remind her we were never raised as siblings. When things were really good and we loved each other as siblings this massive car crash happened. We got so broken and separated and no one ever came along to repair our wounds and put us back together.

You cannot just expect children to be close and love one another because they are born to the same parents. Of course, personality, likes and interests have a huge say in sibling relationships but I work hard to ensure my kids love one another, even when they don't like each other. I have put so much energy into ensuring they know the power and importance of being a good, loyal and loving brother and sister. Would I have done that if I hadn't had my upbringing? Maybe not. Would I have done that if I had always had a positive healthy relationship with my siblings? Maybe not.

People say it's a good thing to experience shit stuff because it makes you pave the way for the future. Sometimes I think I'd have liked the shit stuff to not have happened and this is one example. I see my kids together and I'd have liked to have had the girly chats that Betsy and Lula have as sisters. The age difference between Edie and Betsy is the same as that of my sister and me and I'd have killed to have in her what they have in each other. They have that power in the love they have for one another. It is insane. I don't think that was ever there for us because we were fighting to survive as individuals, me as an infant and my sister as a teenager. Prioritising a sibling relationship wasn't even on the agenda for either of us.

A few years after I had Betsy, when I was still in my early twenties, my mum separated from her partner and returned to live in Devon, a five-minute drive from my house and on the same street as my sister. It was so weird. We had spent twenty years apart; Betsy didn't know her and yet we now saw her every single day.

In the summer of 2020, Lula stayed at my mum's and ended up around one of my siblings. Some stuff was said that really upset her. I voiced to Mum that I was unhappy, she accepted it and promised it wouldn't happen again. The following month I found out from Edie she had planned to spend time with the same sibling. It had been arranged between her dad and my mum. I asked Mum what was going on. She thought Edie would be fine, as she was much younger, so people would know not to talk inappropriately in front of her, but I reminded her Lula was eleven, and should never have heard what she did.

That feeling – when you cannot protect your baby, when you realise you have absolutely no say in what they do because other people – they are in someone else's care – sent me over the edge that day. Those feelings are probably polarised because I was subject to so much hate and horrid conversations when I was growing up. I couldn't cope with the feelings bubbling inside me. I screamed 'FUCKKKKKKK!' down the phone to my mum before I hung up.

Less than a month later, on 1 September, I received a call from Edie's dad. It was 11 p.m. and I was asleep on the sofa. My heart sped up as I answered because it was such an unusual time for him to call. He said, 'I'm just ringing to let you know your mum has throat cancer, so if you want me to have Edie extra days so you can spend more time with her, I can. She's having an operation to remove the cancer next week then her treatment starts.'

I was so confused. I had no clue why he was delivering this news. Josh was next to me, had heard the whole conversation and was equally as confused about why he had made that call. I didn't even answer him. I just hung the phone up. And cried.

I tried calling Mum. There was no answer. I tried again, there was still no answer.

I went to bed but every time I fell asleep I woke up and had that overwhelming feeling of anxiety. My belly was so full of worry and my chest felt tight. It just hit me again and again and again. The next morning I spoke to the kids then I sent Mum a text. I still have it on my phone: 'Mum I got a call last night to tell me you have cancer. I've told the kids this morning as I didn't want them hearing it from anyone else, but they have questions I can't answer and now I've just heard Tallulah crying on the phone to Evie [her maternal cousin] asking if you're going to go bald or lose your voice. I respect your wishes that you didn't want to tell me but I am here if you need me. Take care.'

I heard nothing back.

I called my eldest brother John – he didn't answer. I

called his business partner Paul, and I won't ever forget how decent Paul was to me throughout the next few months and what was to come. He told me my eldest brother had also been rushed to hospital and was really unwell and he wasn't aware about Mum at that time either as he had some tough decisions to make about his own health. I remember just feeling so isolated from it all and like I wasn't part of my family at all anymore.

I tried calling Mum a few more times; she didn't answer and didn't call me back. Shortly after this, one Sunday night, Edie came home from her dad's at teatime as usual. We were sat in the kitchen eating roast dinner. I asked if she had had a nice weekend and she said, 'Yes, I've been at Nanny's with Daddy and his girlfriend all day.' She said they'd spent the day taking care of my mum after the operation to remove her throat cancer. Some of my other siblings were there with them and she told me how poorly my mum was. Mum had stitches covering her entire neck, from her ear across her throat, and she could no longer eat any food. I remember knowing the sick was coming before it arrived. I felt that cold sweat rise up my back and the hairs on my arms stand up, yet I knew I didn't have time to get to the bathroom. I ran to the kitchen sink and just began vomiting in front of Josh and all the kids.

It was total shock. I just had no idea what I had done that was so bad for me to be rejected by an entire family.

They rubbed salt in my wounds by confusing my seven-year-old daughter, taking her to see her nan when she was so ridiculously unwell without me there to explain or make anything better for her.

Edie's dad had never had a real relationship with my mum, not even when we were together, and his girlfriend had not met her before that day. Why anyone would think it was appropriate to spend a day with a woman you don't know who had just had her cancer cut from her throat, was really poorly and had just left hospital was beyond me. I remember feeling, yet again, like I was going mad and I was the one who must be in the wrong. And I felt like I was losing my mind again. I had to, for my own sanity, not respond. Josh was just incredible at breaking all of this down to me and simplifying exactly what was going on around me. He constantly reassured me this was out of my control.

A few months after that I received a call from my brother's business partner. My brother was still unwell and he said, no matter what the rest of my family thought, my mum was still my mum and you only get one mum (a saying that, since undertaking a shitload of trauma therapy, I now hate).

Paul told me Mum was in a bad way, she had lost far too much weight and could no longer keep any food down. That weekend my other family members were going away and she would be home alone, in case I wanted to go and see her. I didn't want to just turn up because I was worried I'd upset her. I was worried they'd turn into a lynch mob if that happened. When I look back, I feel so upset at how fucked up it all was.

I rang her instead – again, no answer. I decided to write her a letter, because despite her clearly not wanting anything to do with me, I didn't want to leave things how they were if the worst was to happen – and it sounded pretty bad. I sat in my car and hand-wrote a letter. It took me almost two hours because I kept stopping. Sometimes my body heaved with sobs and other times I just laid my head back on the headrest looking up to the sky out of the sunroof whilst the tears silently rolled down my face and hit my lap. I felt so many things all at once.

I drove to her house and posted the letter. I suppose, looking back, I was sure she would call and I could go and visit over the weekend and sort things out. Yet she contin-ued to ignore me, as she had since August, when I screamed the word 'fuck' down the phone at her.

I realised I needed help to cope. It was making me poorly to the point that strangers on Instagram were asking if I was OK because I looked unwell and didn't seem myself. I was so emotional all the time, like I had this constant lump in my throat about the 'what if's and I constantly questioned if I was a bad person because of how I was being treated.

Edie was still visiting Mum regularly with her dad and

meeting up with my other family members. She would ask me why I didn't see or speak to certain people and she would question why I was the only one not visiting my mum. I had no control over the situation but she was too tiny for me to go into any detail without making her even more confused or upset. I just had to play it down and pretend it was fine and everyone was happy. I felt so out of my depth. My baby had this other life where she was seeing and speaking with people I didn't want her near. She was being thrown into weird situations that were really confusing but I knew I had to hold it together for her because I had absolutely no idea about how to change or stop it from happening.

Back to fucking therapy I went, to cry and get angry and rant and sob tears of devastation about being the black sheep of the family . . . only, after a few sessions, I realised I wasn't.

I hadn't done anything to be rejected by the entire family. I got angry that someone wasn't nice to one of my children. I was annoyed and frustrated I couldn't make that stop for her. For my baby. My family had then passed the message that my mum had cancer through my ex-partner and he turned into some kind of carer, along with his girlfriend. None of this was anything to do with me. This wasn't a 'me' problem, it was a 'them' problem.

All of a sudden, I was annoyed again rather than devastated. I realised I had reverted back to being a little girl who desperately wanted her mum. It was beyond shit and for the first time I was only angry at myself that my self-worth was on the floor again. So I worked hard on me. I went back to considering my family, my immediate household, the eight of us.

The work I'd put in to ensure we were OK has been relentless for the past eighteen years, since Betsy came along. Every decision I make comes from my childhood, my parents' choices. I overthink, question and dissect everything I do with my kids. For the first time, they were doing it back to me. Questioning why I was so upset over people who I meant absolutely nothing to. People who would have known how their actions made me feel yet did it anyway. My own kids had to educate me, to make me realise I was worth more than the way I was being treated and how it was making me feel. They made me walk away.

One day I was having a chat with Betsy and it just made sense. She said, 'Our family is proper fucked on both sides, isn't it, Mum? I don't see or speak to anyone really on your side and everyone on Dad's side hates me because I stopped seeing him.' It made me feel so sad for her, until she said, 'At least we've changed it, though, because I know my kids will never go through that. They'll have the best nan and grandad and loads of aunties and uncles who love them and loads of cousins they'll see. They won't ever see the fighting and hate we've grown up around.'

As utterly fucking shit as the whole thing was, I realised I'd broken the cycle with my kids. And so I continue to work hard on what goes on in my household, on what goes on with the six people I'm responsible for raising. I want them to see how important it is and how beautiful it is to have that sibling relationship. I see it every day, when Betsy and Seb go for lunch, dinner or out driving together. I see it when Lula and Isaac's friendship groups intertwine and they spend all their time together. I see it when Edie dotes on Wilby twenty-four-seven. I saw it recently when we spent ten days in Mallorca and they dunked each other in the pool, smothered each other in sun-cream and just got each other's jokes and personalities around the dinner table each evening. They have such a fierce loyal love for one another and it's incredible for me to watch.

So I got better. It wasn't a choice any more. When Edie came back from seeing any of them I quickly changed the subject. I blocked anyone associated with them on social media so I didn't see the constant posts on Facebook about my mum's ongoing treatment. Everyone bar me was tagged in helping care for her and I realised I had to keep living for the family I had who loved me. I was so lucky to have them. I had worked my arse off to construct this foundation and it wasn't an option to let it get ruined by anyone.

Months later I was shopping in B&Q when my mum started calling. I felt sick but thought it would be a pocket call so I ignored it. It rang again and again. Josh told me to answer but I couldn't.

Lula called: 'Nan's just called me crying that she needs to talk to you.'

I rang my mum back. She answered and she was sobbing and I couldn't get any sense out of her. She just kept saying, 'I can't do it anymore, Rachaele.'

I drove to her house and it was just heartbreaking to see what cancer had done to her. She was tiny and she was so frail and unsteady on her feet. The part that broke me the most was the state of her flat. She had always been so house-proud. Now she was sleeping all the time in the lounge as her treatment had left her so weak and her sofas were now old and battered.

I took her to DFS and bought her new, comfy sofas that had leg extenders so she could sleep comfortably. I got her a handheld Dyson because she didn't have the strength to hoover with her big model so her carpets weren't in their usual immaculate condition. I knew the mess would be battering her mental health – she didn't even have the physical strength to change her own bedsheets.

I went with a friend and we blitzed the entire flat for a few days. I could see instantly she felt better, although I had this thing going on inside me like a seesaw, up and down, battling with my emotions. On one hand I felt so sorry for her and I wanted to make it all better, but the other part of me hated her for spending seven months ignoring me and allowing the strangest of people into her life to care for her. It was never discussed. We just carried on as if everything was normal, as I've spent the past forty years doing, just rocking around like we have a normal, positive mother–daughter relationship.

We'd go to the garden centre or out for a coffee, making sure she had everything she needed food-wise and whether she could pay her bills. I felt like it was my job to ensure she was OK. But the reality of the 'other people' in my family was very much still there. I wasn't comfortable going round to her house in case they turned up. A lot of the time she was too weak to drive to me. I also had to remind myself that, throughout my life, my mum has broken my heart on more than one occasion without even knowing she had. Yet I still have this tendency to jump straight back in with her every time. I think I'm desperate to have a mum. I know how important I am to my kids, how much they need me every single day. I would kill to have that, but then the reality creeps back in that that's just not us. Devastatingly, since I was four years old, it's never been us.

We lived hundreds of miles apart from one another for twenty years and the fact is, she hasn't ever really been my mum, not consistently. Not perfect, not always getting it right but just to be my mum, through all the good times and the bad. So now we're in touch, but I'm boundaried. I know she still keeps company that to me presents as unsafe and I have to keep myself safe. Every part of me could throw myself back into that relationship. When my mum and I are good it's incredible. Her dry sense of humour makes me cry with laughter and her Mancunian accent will for ever feel like home to me. She feels like home to me and I love being in her company. If you blindfolded me and put me in a room with a thousand women I could still pick her out from her sweet smell alone or the feel of her hands and fingernails. But our relationship is still full of so many tiny broken bits that I know we won't ever be able to glue back together.

I know if I was to go back to contacting her every day, seeing her all the time and doing more with her, the chances are it will go wrong again. It already has once since then, mainly because of other people, rather than her. As she points out to me regularly, she can't deal with arguments or confrontation. I get it because I can't and I'm half her age and physically well but because of that I have to keep my guard up. I imagine that to her at times I feel distant or like I don't care as much as I used to. But I'm this way to protect myself. I can't deal with that level of pain and hurt ever again and, actually, I've come to realise I don't deserve it. No matter what my story was, I didn't deserve it.

Right now, we plod on. Last month she had two bad falls and ended up in hospital. I worry for her health. One of my best friends is a nurse and cares for elderly people on the ward at Torbay hospital and she came to my mum's flat with me after her last fall. Mum was refusing to go to hospital and my friend had a really firm chat with her about ending up in a downward spiral.

I won't lie, it scares me. Sometimes the thought of caring for her going forward scares me more than her rejecting me and me being absent again because now I have to liaise with my siblings. It was fine last week because Mum was well enough to let me know when they were at the hospital and who was taking her home. She ensured we didn't go to her house at the same time, but I know it won't be like this for ever. Just as when I was caring for my nana, her mum, I know the time will come where we all have to care for her and I imagine it will overlap where we have to see each other.

There isn't one part of me that would ever put myself back there after the way they treated me when Mum was poorly. I think about her funeral, which feels shit because she's still here, but she's recently met a funeral director to discuss her options so I know she's thinking about it too. I don't think I would go to her funeral. I feel like that makes me an awful person in one way, but then I think, Who are funerals for? The person you're celebrating has died, they don't know if you're there, and do you really have to stand at a church, at a crematorium or a burial ground to celebrate their life? No.

You can say goodbye from anywhere. I wouldn't want anyone to show up at my funeral if it made them feel anxious or uncomfortable because of other people there. I'd rather they went and sat on a beach alone and raised a glass of fizz or a flask of tea to the sky to remember me. If

I'm honest, writing this feels really shit and awful, because it is, but I'm also aware there are so many thousands of people who follow me who have difficult relationships with their parents and siblings. We all battle over things we can't control and how we will be perceived by other people, most of whom don't really matter in the grand scheme of things. That's why I wanted to raise this, because it is the reality of this thing called life.

Sometimes things are incredible and amazing but sometimes they're just not, and it's about finding a way to navigate through that part, stay strong, focused and to just keep going.

11

THE JUGGLE

Right now, in our home, our weekday mornings are spent getting up and out by 8 a.m. Josh and I have a packed work diary through the week. He spends afternoons and all day Friday with Wilby and I create content for PTWM and Patreon and work at the women's centres, store and distribution centre. It's our normal now to be this busy and our house is chaos most days – a lovely chaos!

It's only when people actually come over and praise us for how well we cope with six kids you actually realise it can be full-on. Six is quite a big number, but we've been doing this for many years now.

In 2015, after the boys came to live with us full-time we were no longer entitled to benefits. I remember going to Lloyds in Torquay to speak to the bank manager (how weird, back when there were so many banks and managers around!) about all the debt I had been landed with. Josh and I were just surviving on our wages and we couldn't afford the repayment of debt. I'll never forget him telling me our country isn't designed to help working families. It would be much more beneficial, he said, for Josh and me to live apart so we could both claim single-parent benefits, then stay together at each other house. We would both get council tax reduction and other's 'benefits' that came from not having a partner. It was the weirdest thing. If I was a single mum I would get way more support than I did trying to hold together my family, work and survive.

We decided that Josh had to pick up as much overtime as possible. It felt pretty crap – his boys were both broken in really different ways. They needed him around as much as possible. But Josh trained in as many specialist skills as possible so he had the chance of getting as much overtime as he could take. This often meant he would be called to do a murder inquiry on one side of the country or police a riot on the other. He was away from home and it meant I tried to manage five babies whilst still going to work. The commute was almost two hours a day each way, by the time I had done the drop-off to breakfast club before school and the pick-up to the childminder's after school. It was exhausting and often felt relentless, but there was never a choice. It was just something we had no option but to do, as do many families, so we could pay the bills, put food in our mouth and pay for their clubs. Seb was semi-pro at football, Betsy was in the gym squad and occasionally we could enjoy the odd luxury.

I felt grateful for Josh, he always just did it. He never moaned or made me feel bad. He was always in awe of how I managed stuff at home. He just worked to the end of each month. When his overtime hit it was worth it for the relief we felt at paying off another chunk of debt, or being able to buy all the kids uniforms without worry at the start of each school year.

When I got my book deal in 2017, I was still working for the same company I'd been with for almost two decades. There had been a recent takeover which meant huge changes and I was in limbo, wanting to leave but the financial security that was tying me there was so strong. In the end we made the choice to go. I had been offered my first advert which paid really well on Facebook, the same amount as I earned in my job for nine months. I figured we had time to find something else. I prayed that I would get some revenue from my book and I was also hopeful I might get more advertising if I could prove I was capable of influencing people with that first advert.

I left my workplace in April 2018. The book was due for release three months later and I was about to go on tour for ten days all over the country to promote it and meet thousands of my followers. It felt really strange going from being regimented with work, having meetings at set times and having to be really structured with my days, to nothing. I only had one advert to film and edit. For the first time in what felt like for ever I got to be a mum – but a happy mum for the first time properly since Betsy was born fourteen years earlier.

The last time I took maternity leave was after I had Edie and during that time I was drowning. It felt so incredible to be in a position to just be a mum. To do actual school runs where I dropped off and picked up the kids from school without rushing rather than frantically throwing them to breakfast club. Arguments stopped instantly and I realised that most were caused by my impatience because I was under so much pressure to ferry five kids to where they needed to be, then get to the office by 9 a.m. It was then that I thought if I was ever in a position to employ my own staff I would without doubt never make them feel that panicked about getting stuck in traffic or having to stay home with their sick child. I realised how stressful the past four years had been whilst I had all of them. I had been a working mum for fourteen years and for the first time I could clean my house whilst the kids were at school, walk the dogs whilst listening to a podcast or drink a cup of tea before it was freezing. It made me see that trying to navigate my way through life had really taken its toll on me. It felt so amazing just to sit, breathe and plan for the future.

I managed to get another advert, then more. My book became a *Sunday Times* bestseller and I was offered a second book to write, this time fiction. It became crazy. I managed things for a year, but after that it was just too much.

I remember the conversation with my therapist in November 2019. I'd had a particularly bad week 'juggling' and I had bawled my eyes out during my session over the pile of dirty laundry I couldn't get on top of. During this time one of my oldest, best friends – who I met at primary school – had begun helping me with all of the campaign stuff I was struggling with. She had a full-time, demanding career herself and she did a few hours each evening helping with the admin side of things. Just those few hours relieved me of so much stress. At that point I was missing emails with fantastic opportunities because I was breastfeeding a baby all day and night. I wasn't getting back to people quickly enough because I was drowning in dirty nappies or rocking a screaming baby round the front room, so they gave jobs to other influencers. Knowing my friend would spend a few hours each evening helping tidy up my inbox, sending invoices, chasing what needed chasing and updating my to-do spreadsheet made me feel better.

My therapist asked why I didn't take my friend on full-time and why I didn't employ a cleaner. I had spent the first half of the session crying about my house being covered in dust, not having the energy to mop sticky floors, empty the dishwasher or clean my bathroom.

I told her that I couldn't justify having a cleaner because I was 'at home' most of the time and I would feel riddled with guilt about what else that money could go on. I'd also have to deal with the feeling I had failed as a mum and wife because I couldn't keep on top of things other mums seemed to be able to. The way she explained it to me made it all so simple.

You see, think of a man who lives in central London and has a fantastic career in the city. He gets to the office early each day to make important calls. If he stays on late because he needs to send an urgent email or secure a deal, we, as a society, would expect him to have a cleaner. In fact, it would be weird for a businessman who works so hard and is career-driven to waste his time doing his own cleaning when he should be working. He's far better placed in the office earning megabucks than running the hoover round, polishing his window sills or changing his own bedsheets. Yet because I am a mum and a wife and I mainly work from my home, it's somehow wrong that the idea of having a cleaner popped into my head. As society expects, I should be able to keep on top of that. The reality, whilst I was running the hoover round and changing the sheets on six beds and a cot each week, was that I was missing emails which meant I wasn't getting really good job offers. I too would have been far better placed answering them so I could earn more money than I would be attending to my home because 'society says so'. It also meant I would be employing an amazing cleaner and would enjoy the opportunity I could offer.

We then spoke about me employing my friend Jo full-time. I explained it was something I would have loved to do but the prospect of her giving up a secure job she had been in for years to work for me was really daunting. I couldn't give any guarantees how long this would last. What if people started to hate me? What if influencing was no longer a thing? What if I had to shut down the page because people no longer found my content interesting, leaving her unemployed? I knew the money I had in the bank from previous ads and the book could last six months and in that time she would be working to hopefully secure us more contracts and deals going forward because she would be focused to do this.

The therapist told me in business things rarely grow unless you take a risk.

I decided to take a risk.

Josh had all the same concerns as me, which made me panic even more. Josh is usually right when things red-flag to him and we were panicking 'about Jo'. All the concerns and worries she was going to have would be even worse because it was her livelihood at stake. By the time she arrived to have 'the chat' with us I thought I was going to be sick.

As soon as I said, 'Would you consider giving up your career and working for me full-time?' she was like 'Yep', no questions, no concerns. She totally believed in us working together and she handed her notice in the next day.

I mentioned the cleaner idea to her but she was like, 'Nah, we can't afford a cleaner just yet. I'll add that into my job description until we're busy enough for me not to have the time to do it.' The naivety, looking back, of how we genuinely worried we wouldn't have enough work to fill her day makes me giggle right now, knowing how Jo's life looks today.

Jo started full-time with me in January 2020. She is one of the kindest, most genuine people I have ever met. In the thirty-five years I have known her, she has never fallen out with anyone. She doesn't do drama or confrontation and she sees the best in everyone, even absolute dickheads. When I tell her the things they've done or ways they've behaved that blow my brain, she will come out with words of advice like, 'Maybe just go grab a Costa with them. Hash it out and try and make peace, life's too short.'

She has always worked in sales and, despite being all of the things in her personal life, with her career she is so on the ball. She is driven, hungry to be the best at what she does and totally willing to go out of her comfort zone and learn new skills.

Three months after she began, we hit the national pandemic and lockdown and I genuinely thought I would have to let her go. She worked, reached out to brands, made relations with PR agencies. It was incredible. She is beyond quick with her turnaround, smashes the best deals and has a full understanding of 'me' so she knows which products to look into and what to turn away. She just gets the job done without any stress or panic being thrown my way and I couldn't have asked for any more.

As soon as she started we sat down and had a lengthy conversation. I asked what she wanted, what her goals were and what her vision was with PTWM. She told me it was her dream to be able to take her daughters to school and pick them up each day. She wanted to manage her hours so they worked for her and her family. She had worked 8 a.m.–6 p.m. for ever and had missed countless sports days and assemblies. She wanted to not have to rely on friends and family members to pick up childcare after school and in holidays. She had been too committed to an office away from home and she wanted enough money to pay her mortgage and bills and get a takeaway each month.

She then asked me exactly the same questions, which I wasn't expecting.

I felt stupid for saying the things I did because I didn't think for one minute they would happen. I told her it was my dream to buy my family a home. I wanted to ensure my friends and family never went without or had to struggle like I once did. More than anything I wanted to open a women's centre, to help people like the me of ten years ago to have a safe hub where any woman and her children can be referred for support.

I was amazed that when I said those things out loud to Jo she didn't make me feel silly, she didn't laugh or roll her eyes like so many other people had. Instead she made notes as I was talking, planned and prioritised jobs. She managed all my money and gave me a 'set monthly wage'. She made me a budget and, behind the scenes, she set money aside so that in less than a year I was able to buy our family a home.

I have been able to treat my family to things. I can bung my friends money when they're struggling and I've been able to replace Josh's mum's cooker and fridge and buy my mum a little reliable car. This was all stuff I have never been able to do before, but Jo also ensured we secured a women's centre. She believed in everything I wanted and she knew, without any doubt, as one of my lifelong best friends and a bloody amazing PA, that we would smash it. In return, as well as her annual salary I put her on commission for campaigns. This meant she's not only been able to pay the mortgage on her family home that was far too small, but she bought a much bigger home which she loves. She's been able to buy herself a dream car and get a takeaway once a month! More than anything it's meant she's been able to do every single school run for her babies and she works from home during all school holidays and manages her own hours so she doesn't have to stress.

The decision to bring Jo on board has changed my family's life. We plan for the future, we have a vision of what we want and we never veer away from that. I know what I want right now, I know what I want for both my social media platforms but also for the women's centre. I remain focused to achieve this constantly. There are a lot of to-do lists. I brainstorm every evening before bed, write lists to clear my mind and I ensure communication in my team is happening daily so we are all on the same page.

12

'INFLUENCING' BEHIND THE SCENES

I know how social media can make influencers look. It's easy to see we get paid fortunes for smiling at the camera, showing off a product and ending with 'Click here to buy'. Whilst I know the money I earn is incredible, I also work, every single day, alongside Jo. Most days she works into the early hours of the morning sending invoices, dealing with PR companies in the USA, editing content or reading through tricky contracts. I know people are interested in the process of influencing as I get asked about it all the time in Q&As.

In August 2022, I signed up to Spotlight Management, mainly because Jo is doing so much work at the centres and in the shop and distribution now. We had plans in the pipeline to do more things PTWM and it was all getting too much. It was a decision we took a lot of time over. Spotlight contacted me originally in August 2021. I turned them down because Jo and I were working really well. I did agree to a call with their CEO and I really liked him. We made an agreement they could bring work to me and if I accepted they would take their commission fee and we would go from there.

In the year that followed Patchwork just got busier and Jo and I were having to turn down really decent jobs Spotlight were bringing to me because Jo had booked stuff. It was clear that Spotlight could bring us the same income and it would halve Jo's workload. What also felt right was I loved the team at Spotlight. They worked in the same way as Jo, in that they didn't sell shit. They are keen to ensure all advertising is authentic and true. They work with decent brands. They always ask me when they get something in and, if it's not something I would use, they just say, 'OK, cool.' They don't pressure me to try, even if it's for a fantastic fee. They know I won't sell or promote anything to do with alcohol or gambling because of the women I support and so I knew it was the best way forward.

Usually a PR company will reach out about a product. Sometimes the brand themselves get in touch but this is really rare. They always ask for recent insights. This is where a lot of influencers don't get work, because they have paid-for followers (or 'bots'). To explain it better, say someone who has a following on Instagram of 100,000 people may have their entire audience engaged. They click the links or @s that they post, etc. Someone who has half a million followers or more may only have forty thousand engaged followers. Even they don't click on links and maybe skip through Stories without engaging with the influencer. Therefore the brand is much more likely to pick the account with the smaller following and offer them more money because they have a genuine, loyal audience. It's no longer about the number of followers you have. It's about the page insights and what that looks like, so the need to have authentic, decent, organic content is something you need to constantly think of.

Occasionally, a big brand will set up a Zoom call to chat through the product and brief the PR company, the influencer and their management. For me, deciding on who I work with is usually a straight yes or a no. There are things I will never sell, but most of these things are also where the big money comes in.

I was offered forty thousand pounds in 2018 to dress up as a fucking poker chip and attend a gambling event at the Dorchester hotel in London and put it on my socials. At that time we were still pretty skint. I had the book coming out but the initial payment wasn't a life-changing sum of money and we still had a shitload of debt to clear. I would stay at a five-star hotel and all travel and accommodation would be paid for. I needed to be there for a minimum of four hours. We could have paid off our debt and had a deposit to move house and get our own mortgage.

But I had lived with a perpetrator who gambled. I can show you the Betfair transactions coming out of my account, day and night, ten pounds here, fifty pounds there. Money I had worked hard to earn to cover food for my daughters or petrol to drive to work was eaten up by a gambler. The highs when he won was like nothing we had ever known. We were all showered in the latest coats and trainers. We went out to eat and could buy something nice for the house. But the lows when he lost were horrific. Football betting on a Saturday used to make me physically unwell because I knew what would happen if he lost. I would sit and watch the TV at home, knowing he would be watching the same match at the pub. I knew he would be running to the bookies at half-time to place another new bet on what team would win and how many goals they would score. If he got it right and won, the whole world felt his happiness and excitement. If he lost, my daughters and I felt his rage. There was no way, absolutely no way I could promote something that I know ruins the lives of so many families.

It's the same with slimming products, alcohol and certain tablets. After I had Wilby the amount of money I was being offered to 'shift the baby weight' was unbelievable and devastating. Whilst women everywhere on Instagram work hard to normalise every type of body shape, companies still profit from making us think we are only worthy if we are slim. Ramming this down the throats of vulnerable, emotional new mums is beyond dangerous.

Jo knows instantly if work will be a yes or a no. She will always run it past me but it comes down to the fact I either use it or I don't. If it's something she thinks I might like, for instance, a natural deodorant, hair or skin product, we will accept products to trial. We make a decision on whether we will enter into a paid campaign with them after I've used their product. Often this is a no. We once received a blender when Wilby was weaning and I just couldn't work it. I couldn't get the lid on, I couldn't purée the food with ease. One day the whole fucking thing exploded and my kitchen was covered in runny apple and pears. I was just like, 'JO, FUCK THIS.'

I cannot and will not sell a product I don't believe in, because chances are you will feel the same. Then you won't trust me and I will sell fuck-all going forward and I won't get any work. I see it constantly. I've met other influencers at events who would sell their own nan if the price was right. In the end it will only affect them. I know this because I'm influenced myself. There are certain influencers I watch and I buy their stuff and it's ace. I have bought everything this summer for Wilby that Mrs Hinch has bought for Ron, because I know she's genuine, despite what the twats on the internet say about her. She could do so many more adverts. She could be on TV and in magazines. I know from my management team that she is the most powerful influencer. She could earn triple what she takes now but she sticks to what she loves. Because of that people buy into her and to date there isn't one product she's recommended that I've bought and thought, That's a load of shit.

So, once you agree on a product you talk money. This is something I never get involved with. I would struggle to haggle over a leather belt in a Turkish market so the thought of selling myself for the highest price knocks me sick. I'm also really grateful to receive the money I get paid so I'd likely take the first (and far too low!) offer. This is where Jo came in and now, even better, my management team. Because they manage loads of talent they know without question what a campaign is worth and what we should be getting paid. If a brand won't pay it they just decline without question. I get so panicky when this happens but they are literally like, 'No, Rach, something better will come along' and to date it always has.

Once we agree the price we get the contract. This is where having management helps again. Some contracts are hefty documents full of tricky language and it takes time to dissect them. Occasionally this is where we change our minds and pull out because the exclusivity rights or paid spend they want behind products just isn't worth the fee they're paying. For instance, we had a chocolate brand try to insist that I couldn't work with any other chocolate company for twelve months. I love chocolate and I eat all kinds of brands and types so it doesn't make sense for me to sign a year of my life away for one paid advert. Again, so many influencers have come unstuck here, especially within the cleaning community. They start out building their accounts, showing a variety of brands of cleaning products which people engage with, then they get a brand deal for one particular brand and before you know it they have to change their whole page. They can only advertise one brand of cleaning products and people don't engage as much as it doesn't feel as authentic. And the reality is that we all use loads of brands of everything – whether it's shampoo, toilet roll or toothpaste. Most of the time people go with what's on offer, or what they're influenced to buy!

We then get the brief and product. Jo and I turn that into a script for the content. We film, we post and we send feedback.

And that's it.

The life of an influencer.

So that's what we do all year and this year I've also been hands on in the women's centre working with the women which I love, plus writing this book!

Jo and I take ten days off at Christmas and this year we've both holidayed abroad for a week to ten days but other than that we have worked every day. It's been flat out to the point I needed that cleaner much sooner than we ever could have hoped for. Rather than feeling guilt and shame about having her I felt proud. Needing someone to help me manage my home because I am busy with a career I love is a huge achievement, even if society doesn't agree.

Fuck society.

The bigger point is what it has enabled me to do.

13

THE WOMEN'S CENTRE

After I left my employment I became a patron for an incredible charity in Plymouth called Trevi. Trevi works with women in recovery and is passionate about giving them the best chance possible to help them heal and remain with their children. Watching what they did, speaking to the staff and meeting and interviewing the women there left me in awe.

If every human got a chance to go to Trevi and listen to the women's stories it would change the way society views so many things. It would also make people much kinder and far less judgemental. The path most of those women have had to walk is quite honestly soul-destroying and it made me want to do more.

At the same time, I began working with Women's Aid on some of their campaigns and then Refuge got in touch. I got involved with one of their campaigns on tech abuse and travelled to London for their bittersweet, fiftieth anniversary. The work both of those domestic abuse charities do and the stats they regularly share are utterly devastating. After the work I had done during lockdown with Nina locally on the community fridge I made the choice I had to do more within my local area.

Jo and I made a plan. If we could save enough money from my Part-Time Working Mummy income to ensure we had enough funds to pay for a small building to rent for a year, along with staff and running costs, we would take the leap. In 2021 we secured our first building. We rented it thinking we could just give it a lick of paint, lob some plants and wall art up and we would be good to go but it ended up being an absolute shitshow. There was rising damp, everything needed replacing from the electrics to the plumbing and there was no hot water. We needed to install a fire system and we had to buy everything from a kettle to a washing machine. We had to replace all the flooring because of the damp.

We spent thousands of pounds we weren't expecting to spend. The number of times I battled Josh and Jo and promised them to just believe in me was really hard some days. Mainly this was because I was battling in my own brain wondering if I had made a huge fucking mistake, and convincing myself I was still doing the right thing always felt harder. We opened the door six months later and I won't lie: there have been teething issues.

All I wanted was a safe, homely space where families could come to collect food parcels, do their washing free of charge, use our phone and internet and get support and advice. What we now offer is much more than that because the need to grow was huge. I opened a second, much bigger centre in 2022. We managed to get some funding; however, a lot of the time you have to provide twelve months of bank statements. I needed an income stream for us that was guaranteed. I needed to take the financial weight off my shoulders because I had sunk tens of thousands into the centre already. In March this year we opened Patchwork the store, an online shop and a store front next to our Paignton women's centre where we sell our own merchandise and wholesale other small businesses. All of the profit from sales goes into the women's centres.

Last week we had a meeting with DPD, as we thought about switching our courier service. The sales lady came out and wanted to look at what we do as you have to be sending a certain amount of packages for them to work with you. She was in shock at what we've already achieved in the short time we've been open. She told the staff she has never seen sales like it from a start-up and our turn-over in the first six months is like nothing she's ever seen. It made me feel proud, not only of the girls I employ and how hard they work to ensure we get this income but also of myself. I set up that shop so the profit would go straight into the centres, not to me personally. Every bit of profit we make sits in the Patchwork account. It pays for food so local families can eat, it funds courses that are facilitated by qualified people which are crucial to helping the women we support. It covers rent, utilities, staff wages and training.

To date, all I have done with Patchwork is add money when we've struggled financially. I eat, sleep and breathe Patchwork and I have since the day it opened. I deliver training to women. I am in all the buildings most days, so I see all of the staff in the shop, distribution area and the centres. I ensure they feel supported and valued. I come up with ideas to help us be more sustainable until, hopefully, we can get more funding and grants to do work within our town.

There isn't any other service that does anything like we do. When I was umm-ing and aah-ing about leaving my perpetrator so many years ago, it would have massively helped my girls and me if we had been told about my centre and I had gone along and been met by women who had lived experiences. They would have greeted me without judgement and showed me support and understanding. I could have been offered a domestic abuse course whilst I was still with my perpetrator, in secret. I would have learned about types of abuse, the damage it was causing to my children and me and how I could leave as safely as possible. We would have left much sooner. I would have realised my worth far quicker and I wouldn't have spent a decade of my life living with abuse.

My dream is to keep growing.

Knowing your worth

Devastatingly, I could open a centre in every surrounding town tomorrow and they'd be full to capacity within six months because the world is in a shit state. Services which are life-saving are being cut every single day. There are so many dreams I have, women of all ages I want to support by doing different things.

I am desperate to get into secondary schools and work with girls who feel they don't fit in. Having been a girl in secondary school and having had a daughter go through it, another one there now and Edie due to start soon, the struggles are still apparent and worse still due to social media. I have friends whose teenage daughters feel they don't fit in and they're so lost. They hate school to the point it makes them really poorly. I want to create a safe space where all the lost girls can come together, where they can journal, do mood boards for their futures and have somewhere lush and cosy where they can all hang out and support one another and see there is more to life than secondary school.

When you are desperately unhappy, in any situation, at any age, it's incredibly hard to envisage 'life after this' because you're in survival mode. You're fighting like fuck just to get through your days. We struggle as adults during bad times to stay positive enough to think we will get through it. Teenage girls should be taught that there is a whole world after they walk out those school gates, and actually what they're feeling and enduring at that time will one day be nothing but a distant memory. It's our duty to validate their feelings about how hard school is, but also to plot and plan their futures with them, focus on their dreams and goals, get them around other girls who feel equally as lost, worried or as angry at the world as they do. We should encourage friendships outside the one place they hate and have to spend the majority of their teenage years in.

I want to start clubs for older women. This week I saw a lady in her sixties who had been kicked out of her family home by her perpetrator and had her adult children alienated against her. I asked her about her childhood. She told me it was 'good' and that she got the occasional clip round the ear off her nan when she was naughty. I asked why her nan smacked her rather than her parents and she told me her dad had left when she was young. Her mum had entered into a relationship with a guy who beat them both regularly, so at the age of nine she went to live with her nan because it was safer than staying.

Let's dissect this – here you have a little girl, who's abandoned by her biological dad, mum gets a new partner who beats shit out of her and her mum, she then has to live apart from Mum and goes to live with her nan. She smacks her when she displays any kind of emotion she can't handle. I live for those lightbulb moments. I live for that moment when I point the parts to women that are utterly horrific and yet because of society they never saw what they'd endured.

There is so much stuff right now that you can't see until you're in it. People cannot make it better because no one knows it exists. Take one woman we support. She was born into a huge family, she was sexually abused in her family home and she told authorities. Because she spoke up, all her siblings were told by the parents that their being split up and experiencing huge intervention from authorities was her fault. She is now a young mum, an adult. She has minimal support around her and is financially struggling. Yesterday, I went to her house to deliver a food parcel. When she came to the door she couldn't hold it together. She desperately needs to see a dentist and told me she didn't have one. She also didn't have credit on her phone or any internet. I told her to leave it with me. I went back to the centre and called my friend who is a dental hygienist. She told me NHS dentists were no longer taking new patients on but I could try the local emergency dentist. They told me they get over forty calls a day from people in severe pain without a dentist and can only see around ten. By this point my brain ached.

The woman was told she would have to contact her GP to be referred to them and they 'may' be able to see her. Her GP practice sent a text message to her that read exactly: 'Due to unforeseen circumstances, we have a shortage of GPs available. Wherever possible please try alternatives such as 111, pharmacy and NHS online.'

Now I was feeling all kinds of things here and I am a happily married, financially stable woman surrounded by support who has a fuck-ton of therapy to help me manage my emotions. I looked at this beautiful, broken girl in front of me and I just thought, once again, How is this fair? She is never going to be able to manage this situation because it's so absolutely overwhelming. Every way she turns no one can help her and she's just being sent from pillar to post with zero support or care. She's brimming with anxiety, she is in pain and she just needs someone to help her but it's not out there.

There are so many times I have wanted to scream and shout and cry and rage at other services or people because of the things they do to the women we support – or, very often, don't do.

We regularly get asked if we have space to supervise contact (put in place usually when families are in crisis or children have been removed from their parents' care) at one of our centres. Our town had one building when we started out where most supervised contact was being held. Isaac had to see his mum in 2015 in a contact centre when he was first removed, at that time a huge church in Torquay town centre where lots of families sat and played with their children every Saturday between 10 a.m.–12 p.m.

The boys' mum had to turn up early to wait, then we would drop Isaac off, collect him at 12 p.m. and she would wait in a room until we had left then she would come out. After a while that contact centre shut and the closest one was a place called Little House, Exeter. We then had to get to that every Saturday morning. This was over an hour away from our house in the traffic at that time.

People who use contact centres are usually parents who have had their children removed. They get to see them in these buildings when their children have been placed with another relative or if they have been placed in foster care. Many of the women we support live with addiction or domestic abuse. They are trying to get their children back to live with them if they have been removed through the family court. They may have recently had their children placed back in their care but have to get to the contact centre for their children's dad to see the children under supervision.

We have had so many women who have shown us their court orders which are just heartbreaking because, currently, they're just set up to fail.

Let's imagine you are the mum who has just had her children returned to her from foster care. They were removed because there was domestic abuse in the household that their dad was perpetrating. It was stated their mum couldn't protect them. You (mum) has ended her relationship with their dad and is also trying to live without alcohol as she's been in addiction for many years. She has now been clean, let's say, for six months and her court order states she needs to get to the contact centre so her kids can see their dad. Let's say her kids are small – a baby and a three- and five-year-old. I want you to picture this in your brain as if you, yourself were trying to do this.

She doesn't drive, no one is available to give her a lift and it's winter – cold and wet. She gets on the bus, it takes half an hour to get there and when she arrives the contact centre is another long walk as it isn't on the bus route. She walks there with all the children. They're tired and cold and refusing to walk; she's trying to push a pram and carry the others so they get there on time, otherwise she will be in trouble for not adhering to her court order. She arrives just in time, the baby is scream-ing and clinging to his mum as he doesn't want to be handed over to a total stranger. She then leaves, and she can still hear the baby crying. She has to then find some-thing to do whilst her kids see their dad for the next hour and a half. There's nothing to do. There is nothing close by and she's freezing and emotional.

She hangs around, then goes to collect the kids at the correct time. The three- and five-year-old are really upset because they miss their dad. She can't calm them down.

The baby is tired, hungry and unsettled and she has to walk back to the bus in the rain. It's now even colder and pitch black. (Just picture this, take a minute to think how she's feeling.) The two eldest (but still extremely tiny) children can't regulate their emotions but she doesn't have time to find a cafe (not that she can afford a drink or snack with the cost of living) because her court order states she now needs to attend another meeting on the other side of the town.

She then has to try and get back on the bus and travel almost an hour in the other direction and, if she doesn't, she will be at risk of losing her children again. As part of her court order she had to have a new scram bracelet fitted. This measures her alcohol consumption to ensure she isn't drinking. Imagine trying to do this with three tiny, inconsolable children. She then has to get back on the bus to get to where she lives, which, by the way, is likely to be temporary accommodation. This is where most of the women we support are housed. This isn't a cute cosy new build we are led to believe women get, or a safe women's refuge, no. This will be a huge block of flats where she will be housed with other people, including men (who she's absolutely petrified of) still living with addiction, families being subjected to domestic abuse which she will hear and see and others living with mental health issues. How utterly terrifying, triggering and devastating.

I look at that and I think, Could I do it? Could I get three small children around my local town to contact, meetings and home – and I drive and I am well and happy. Could I then do it if I was a recovering alcoholic having just fled domestic abuse, having only just had my children returned to me from foster care with minimal support around me?

The chances are I couldn't. The chances are most of these women are going to fail and that's not because they're not trying or they don't want it enough. It's because a lot of the time the people in charge of putting stuff in place make it absolutely impossible. You will pass other women every day who live terrible lives like this, you will also be surrounded by women and children who are being subjected to domestic abuse.

Hundreds of thousands of women who we work along-side, deliver our babies, teach our children, write our prescriptions, appear to be fine, intelligent, happy and succeeding. Some probably believe they are, but once you pick that scab you realise they're in such pain, they're broken – delightfully broken. The whole point of the women's centre, the reason I opened it, is to help them firstly recognise what they are going through, then work to repair their wounds and help them to heal until they shine like a star.

There is no greater feeling for me than working with families at our centres. I love getting in there, mopping the floors, brewing the tea. Colouring in lions with little boys and reading books to little girls, listening to all their hopes and dreams and making them believe they're all achievable . . . I watch their mums walk through our door and every part of their body language screams how much they don't want to be there. Months later they stroll out, with so much self-worth, a little tool kit to help them cope and a bucket so full of love and support that they just smash the shit out of life. It is without doubt my happy place, even on the bad days, sometimes more so on the bad days, because they're the days I imagine us not being there: where would these women and children go then?

I have asked a few of our women to write some testimonials, which they did in September 2022. I have chosen to share two with you below with the permission of the ladies who wrote them. We started supporting both of these women less than three months ago and the work they have done on themselves, the changes in their lives because of that is just incredible.

I first entered the Patchwork House with very low expectations, very low self esteem and very little hope. The hour I shared with two exceptionally kind, knowledgeable and supportive women in there changed my life. I left feeling I did have hope and I found people who believed me and believed in me.

I felt inspired by the ladies I met that day, fierce survivors themselves who were able to gently and expertly guide me through the support they could offer me, showing genuine kindness and understanding, relating elements of their own experiences and imparting a sense that I would be OK. This was not a feeling I had dared consider prior to the first meeting I had at Patchwork House.

The space itself is pretty quirky and comfortable, not a dull generic therapy space. This in itself helped me feel cared about. Thought has obviously gone into creating this environment which offers visitors the sense that they matter and are valued.

As well as providing a safe supportive place for me to share my experiences I was given valuable practical advice, a freedom course book to take away and, most importantly, a sense of not being alone. I had subsequently revisited and was signposted to a six-week course which The Patchwork House runs which has provided me with a toolbox of knowledge and techniques to empower me to move forwards.

I cannot thank The Patchwork House enough. I now feel able to start piecing my life together as a single mum of very young children against a back catalogue of a coercive, controlling relationship which has left a significant shadow across my children and my life.

Without the practical and optional support provided by The Patchwork House my journey would be considerably more difficult and I know I would not have been able to join the dots myself to understand how to start moving past feeling defeated.

Thank you Patchwork x

I was referred to Patchwork House earlier this year when I was struggling with my mental health due to the constant harassment and abuse I was receiving constantly from my ex-partner and father of my small child.

The first time I arrived at Patchwork I was physically trembling, I couldn't catch my breath to explain what was happening because I was so emotional and anxious.

Rachaele and Jane sat and took their time, they calmly explained to me all about domestic abuse, I began to see that everything my ex-partner was doing was still extremely controlling and they gave me support to put immediate boundaries in place as I thought, because of our child we share together, he 'had' to be able to contact me as and when he wanted.

As soon as I put those boundaries in place it was like a weight had been lifted and I could finally breathe for the first time in a long time.

The Patchwork Team then encouraged me to apply for a local job, helping me write a job application to the hospital. They helped me sort out a council tax debt that my perpetrator had left me with that I had ignored for so long because I couldn't face it. I am now on an affordable payment plan.

They gave me weekly food parcels and rather than the basic food we usually had from food banks they popped a few treats in for my toddler and some fresh healthy bits and fruit and veg so I could cook us proper meals, as well as sanitary wear and toiletries which I struggle to afford with the current cost of living.

They then gave me a place on their trauma course, I am now two weeks in to a six-week course with a qualified hypnotherapist that helps us to look at our brain pathways, the science behind what we do and a toolkit to help us cope going forward, the change to me already is life-changing.

Before I went into a relationship with my perpetrator I was a keen cook, I was passionate about food. I have spoken with Patchwork about whether I could volunteer when I leave their service to help other women understand about different foods, their benefits and how to make and cook healthy tasty meals on a budget, they are really keen for me to do this and are speaking with Trevi charity in Plymouth who do a similar project to see if this is something we can make happen in Torbay.

I am forever grateful I found Patchwork House.

Before I found their service I was in a downward spiral where my anxiety and depression was having a negative impact on both my daughter and yet now I feel positive, I know the 'bad feelings' will pass and I am excited for the future of my daughter and I for the first time in a long time.

And these are the bits I take, the testimonials, the happy tears, the beam on their faces when they get their certificates for completing one of our courses. I have to remember we can't solve everyone's problems or fix every woman who walks through our doors at Patchwork but there are many who we can make things better for. There are hundreds of women who we have been able to support who have gone on to achieve incredible things, even if that's getting out of bed in the mornings and realising they are worthy of living.

There is honestly nothing like it. You see the transition from the women who walk in to meet us to the same women saying goodbye a few months later. It's incredible and I hope we can continue for as long as it's needed . . .

14

FINDING ME AGAIN

I realised because of the years of trolling I had lost my way a little, so I decided to open up a Patreon account where people could subscribe for five pounds a month and get access to a private Instagram account where I could be 'me' again.

It worked – pretty quickly.

To sign up to Patreon people had to use a debit card or PayPal address which meant if they went on to troll me on there I would be able to identify them. To date there has been one troll who voiced their hatred of me. I kicked them out and blocked them. Of course, there are other trolls on there. I know this because they screenshot the content and post it elsewhere. But other than that there are almost three thousand of us now and it's a proper community. Everyone is just lush. It was my original plan when I set up to do Stories and posts about the things I had lost my confidence with over at PTWM. Actually, the reactions I received, the amazing feedback I got, has meant I now do regular Lives where we all chat and hang out – the people on there also chat to one another. I do a monthly podcast, a wellbeing podcast, Instagram Lives and regular Q&As. It's just given me back me, the me I was before the nameless, faceless accounts stole a little part of me.

It has also given me the confidence to be more me back on PTWM because I realise that actually there is far more good than bad, and the people that are good are just bloody lush and kind and funny! I love being on Patreon. I never get the worried tummy flips or tight chest when I'm on there. I don't get the dread when I see a flurry of messages hit my inbox and when I do a Q&A all the questions are always asked from a place of genuine intention. The issue was I was spending more time on Patreon and less on PTWM. Jo and my management kept reminding me that the money sits with PTWM, so it underlined how much I needed to be present on my channels.

I also had the two women's centres, the online and store front opening and, before I knew it, I was employing nine staff. The overwhelm that comes with that – knowing nine people rely on me to pay their rent, mortgages and bills – is sometimes really tough. I was stretching myself everywhere within the centres and shops because I wanted to be involved. I needed to know everyone had the same vision and I also wanted to be visible. I wanted them to feel supported and that they had me there to bounce ideas off.

I was then still busy with adverts, this book was being talked about, I had two social media platforms to run, and I was contacted by the family courts to work with them on how they tackle domestic abuse and support victims and survivors within their service. I also still worked with the charities I'd been involved with and, above all, I still had six babies who relied on me to prioritise them.

With everything we had going on with Wilby when he got his diagnosis, it made no sense for Josh to be working as he was. By this time, he was in a really demanding role within the police force, which he absolutely loved. It meant he needed to be focused and give it a lot of his attention. He made the choice to go on a career break. I said 'No' at first. We would manage with him still working because I know how much he loved his job. I also worried about how he would cope after being in such regimented careers for the last twenty years with the army and the police force. He hadn't ever really seen what my work looked like, the same as I never saw his. On the odd occasion I would chat to one of his colleagues or read a newspaper article about a job he had been involved with. I would beam with pride but we were both so busy within our own careers we never knew what each other's days looked like – and mine were messy.

No day is the same. Some days I work back-to-back with women at the centre. I deliver a domestic abuse course and I argue with housing officers and landlords and meet with social workers. I go and view flats or run food parcels round the bay all day. At Christmas I dress as an elf and spend twelve hours driving round, handing out presents to kids who would get nothing otherwise. Other days I am in back-to-back Zooms with my management team and brands and being filmed in a supermarket showing the latest deals. One week I may need to go away to work with a charity I support in London and then I lock myself away in my bedroom to write three chapters for my book. At the same time I try and fit in school runs and cooking chicken pasta – the only dish that my kids love me for! I wondered how Josh would cope being around this. For Jo and me, it's fine. This is our life. We thrive off busy, crazy, stressful days on which we skip lunch, never drink enough water and always end with, 'We'll do that tomorrow.'

Josh likes structure and he lives for routine. He starts with the gym at 5 a.m., eats three meals a day, snacks on berries and nuts and always drinks enough water. I worried our worlds might collide . . . but he was adamant. It was physically impossible for me to manage and right now, and for the foreseeable, our youngest baby needed us around. He needed a routine and we were in a place financially where Josh could remain within the force but take a break from his career. He could give our family more of his time.

His career break began at the beginning of June 2022. We're a few months in and I cannot tell you how incredible it has been having him around.

He's taken on so many little roles within the business that were just not being dealt with. He has helped us to make decisions about where to cut back and where to grow and we've just taken on another new member of staff. Josh's approach is different but in a good way, and when he deals with tricky stuff there is no agenda. He just does it because it needs doing, because he is assertive and just tackles stuff head on without the worry and panic that tend to consume me.

Right now, it feels like he was the missing jigsaw piece. I didn't know it was missing until he came on board but he has brought much more structure and calm into my days. I feel less stressed now. I know where I'm at ahead of time because he sits with Jo and me every Monday morning and we plan and prep for the week ahead. I am really keen to have staff on both Part-Time Working Mummy and Patchwork who share my vision. I want to work with those who just get it and have that passion to do what we're doing and know why we're doing it. At the same time I want to be in the thick of it for the foreseeable.

I remember my managing director at the care company

I worked at coming on site visits with me. We would meet at one of our homes where we housed adults with autism and challenging behaviour. We had homes all over Devon, Plymouth and Surrey, we had hundreds and hundreds of members of staff and he was at the top of the chain. He was the CEO of a multi-million-pound private care company. But when we walked into any of those homes he would do whatever needed doing. He would see a full bin and take the rubbish out. He would run the dishcloth over the worktop in the kitchen and he would put the kettle on for the staff. I always remember that about him. He wanted to know everyone – the clients we cared for and the care staff who worked for us. He would get to know everyone as well as he could and he would stop and chat to people. I always saw how many people were shocked that someone who held such a huge role within a company was just so normal and decent.

It made staff feel seen. He gave them a space where their opinions and ideas were valued and heard and he taught me so much about how we should treat people. So that's why I need to be in amongst it all. I want my staff to see I see them, to know how much I appreciate them. Like how I parent when I revisit parts of my childhood to get it right, to be the best employer I go back to when I was an employee. What did I need from my bosses? I needed them to see I worked hard, I needed flexible working so I could pick stuff up in the evenings or at weekends which meant I could attend sports day or parents evening. I needed support during school holidays as I had to co-parent with an ex who could be narcissistic and abusive. And you know, so much of that was never met. After our company was bought out and I got a whole new management team, things changed and I spent so many days feeling physically unwell with anxiety. What would happen if I was sick, or if I had to take time off because my kids were poorly? I dreaded organising childcare within the school holidays as I knew my ex would make it as difficult as he could and I would not get child-care. There was the risk the children would be collected late, making me late. All of those things were out of my control yet they had such a detrimental effect on my mental health because I had employers who expected me to work in an office at certain times and I was subject to disciplinary procedures if I couldn't manage their expectations.

My staff manage their own diaries. They're visible to us all so we can see each other's whereabouts but if they need to work from home they can, doing Zooms or an extra week when their kids are at school. Taking time off in the holidays is fine. If their kids are poorly they take the day off to care for them without question. Family and mental health first. I will support them as best I can and you know what? In return I have the most dedicated, hard-working team. They are in group chats in the evenings, at weekends. They go above and beyond what they're expected to work and the support they show one another when they're going through shit times is incredible. I am in the thick of it with them, so they know I value them, I see and hear them and I love it. I love working in the shop and meeting people who have travelled for hours to come and visit. I love hearing their stories and chatting to them. I love hanging out with Jen in the distribution centre, watching her package parcels that people have bought to support us. I love her showing me her new website ideas or asking me if I like the new marshmallows we've just begun stocking. I love delivering the freedom programme and seeing the change in so many women. I love meeting with other services and working out what we can do within our community to support one another. I love getting us all together to hang out and bring loads of different ideas and thoughts to the table. We all encourage and praise one another. I love everything Patchwork!

I won't lie. In an ideal world, I would deactivate my account and just spend for ever hanging out with my Patchwork team because the internet at times makes me unhappy. But then I get a bit of courage to write something from my heart and post it. It's not often any more, because I think that love for it never really came back after the trolls took it away. That passion at 4 a.m.: I would wake from a dream and just start typing in the dark, but that disappeared in 2019. Yet every now and then I will open up my notes, I'll type my thoughts and feelings on something, find a picture to match and pop a post on Instagram.

Only last week I posted about the challenges and joy of Wilby starting preschool and I was met with tens of thousands of the most incredible, heartwarming reactions. People commented, liked and shared my post, they inboxed me so much love, followed with their own stories. Josh will say, 'See, you can still do it,' and I think, I'm going to write more, but then a new referral will come into Patchwork that's urgent or Jen will have a batch of fudge that she's stocking that I need to try or I need to grab a shop for the centres as we're out of food and time just flies.

I suppose reflecting on it now, I think, Do I miss it? Yeah, in a way, I do. Because I'm good at it, and it takes a lot for me to admit to being good at stuff. Whenever we get in a black cab in London and the taxi driver always asks what we're there for I *always* give Josh 'the look' because he always says, 'We're here for meetings for my wife's work.'

Then they say, 'Oh, what do you do?'

And my belly flips because the words 'social media influencer' knock me sick and whenever I go to say, 'Author,' I feel like I have imposter syndrome. Despite (soon to be) three published books, two of which are *Sunday Times* bestsellers, I still can't call myself an author out loud, but for years Josh has. He shouts from the rooftops about my work, my books and my centres. He is so ridiculously proud of me and it's something I wish I'd had as a child.

I wish I'd have had someone who was proud of me, who told me my English homework was good, because it always was. I was always top set in English and I loved it. The feelings I get from Josh being proud of me in the last eight years has made me see why it's crucial our kids know we are proud of them. It is life-changing for everyone to have 'a person' as I mentioned earlier. Just one person to cheer you on and make you believe you can achieve all your hopes and dreams.

So, maybe I'll write again, maybe I'll write more. Maybe the next time I wake at 4 a.m. with a story my brain wants to tell, I will actually write it down and hit 'post', who knows? But for now, I remain here, juggling social media platforms, women's centres, book-writing and raising babies. And I have Josh around much more to help support our children, who are all individually on the rollercoaster that is life.

15

THE FUTURE

So for now that's our life. People constantly ask us what our future looks like but it's absolutely impossible to know.

Who'd have thought in 2016 when I wrote that first Facebook post it would have led to three published books, two women's centres, an online store and a shop front! I would love to say I have a plan, but the reality is I just keep going. I chase my dreams and I work hard to make them happen. That passion to reach people in my community, that need to ensure no woman feels like I did when I fled our home twelve years ago is still as strong today as it was back then. Now I know you can not only get through it, you can succeed. You can go on to achieve all your goals and dreams and you can be happy. I need to be out there, ensuring other little girls like Betsy and Tallulah have a safe space to come to where they will be seen and their mums get the care and support they need.

For now, I continue on social media. I often talk about the day I disappear off the internet at home to the kids and Betsy always says, 'Mum, these people have been in my life since I was twelve. It's not fair to come off the internet. They wanna see how my life pans out and I want them here for that.' It makes me laugh.

It's crazy to think it's only been six years since we opened parts of our lives up to the world. It feels much longer most of the time. It's been a long six years and it's very much a learning curve as to what we show and share, as you can see! A love–hate learning curve, a lot of the time.

And Josh has just under five years at home with us until his career break ends. Then he has to make the decision to return to Devon and Cornwall as a police officer or resign and hang out with us for longer. Who knows where we will be when that time comes, or what he will choose to do? You'll have to watch this space!

What I do know is I constantly feel grateful and fortunate, even on the bad days. Even when I sob on the end of my bed because the kids have sent me over the edge, work feels too overwhelming or someone has trolled me hard on the internet that day, I still never forget where I came from. Even the bad days now are better than the good days before this life. I am safe and I am loved and that is something women I meet every day dream of. For the first thirty years of my life I would have cut my arm off to have that feeling.

I am excited for our future.

I read an article the other day in which a lady had written an open letter to her husband. They have three young children, all under the age of five, and she spoke of how tough it was. What she said really got me. She was explaining to her husband how they should cherish these moments whilst their children are tiny. She said something along the lines of, 'I know it's noisy day and night but one day our home will be silent. I know they shout our names a hundred times an hour but one day they'll be grown up and gone and we will go days, maybe longer, without hearing from them.'

She went on to say that they had so much to look forward to because they will fall in love for the third time when their children leave home. She said they fell in love for the first time when they met and did so much together, they fell in love again when they had children and their lives changed and they still have a third time to fall in love when the children grow and leave home. I realised Josh and I never got that first time. When we met we already had children and we never really got any time for just us. The minute we announced our relationship we were in the trenches. We constantly had children and rarely got time to just be 'us'.

We missed out on stuff other couples take for granted: the cinema dates, weekends away, dinners out and lazy beach days. From day one we had a tiny baby to consider with Edie. We were fighting to make it work from the get-go and, as incredible as it still felt, I'm sad we never got time for each other, time to just lazily fall in love. But we got the second time and I'm excited for the third.

I'm excited for the eight of us and whoever else they bring into our lives along the way, for us to grow alongside one another.

I cannot wait to see what my children go on to do, what makes their hearts happy and I also know there are gonna be many more times I'm going to catch them when they fall, and that's OK too. I'm quite good at catching.

I just wanted to say thanks to you, reading this, for supporting me. If you are nice to me on the internet or in real life you have no idea of the impact that has in my life. Even if you picked me up off a shelf in a charity shop or on your holiday – thanks for sticking with it and getting this far!

I feel I should probably end this book the same way I ended the first, because even though we're half a decade on, there is still is a sentence that sums up life so well. So take care of yourself, always look for those little bits in every day that make it worthwhile and remember – everything is temporary.

ACKNOWLEDGEMENTS

To my babies – all six of you – this eighteen-year journey that they call motherhood has been the wildest ride of my life. Thank you for making me smile and laugh until I cry and for showing me that every day is a learning day, but, most of all, thank you for making my heart feel things that I didn't know were possible.

To Josh: thank you for being the first person to love me in my whole life, consistently and unconditionally. The three decades I spent before you came along taught me that what we have together is better than a lottery win.

To my friends – the ones who still exist in the circle that's now almost the size of a full stop! – thank you for sticking by me. Because of the lessons we've learned in the last five years, we are now more fierce than ever, together. I am forever grateful to you all for reminding me about what and who is important. For having my back, you will forever have my heart. I love you all.

To my Patchwork team: thank you for supporting my vision, for never making all of my dreams, plans and goals seem impossible, even if at times you probably feel like they are. What we have achieved for women and children in our community in the past two years is the stuff of miracles.

To my mum: I'm so proud of how you've smashed your fight with cancer despite it being one of the most brutal, gruelling journeys. I still wish, far too often, that on that day in 1986 when you got in your car and drove off, I was sat next to you. I love you very much.

To Jo: thank you for making everything I've written here possible. Everything I am is because you're beside me, guiding me and having difficult conversations with me for which I'm forever thankful. Thank you for making my dreams come true – I love you!

To Mummy Marshall: for just being you. Every time I bury my face into you, it smells like home. Thank you for accepting me and loving me as hard as you do.

To my management team at Spotlight: thanks for not only looking after my workload but for looking after my wellbeing. You checking in, praising me and listening to me never goes unnoticed.

To my editor, Emma – my very first editor in 2018 and now once again. I am so chuffed you found me.

Thank you for allowing me to run with this book as I wanted and for always just getting it, just getting 'me'. You're the best.

To Jo, my incredible, lush, happy, smiley literary agent. You forever make me giggle every time you lob in an accidental swear word over a Zoom call. Thanks for ensuring the very best for me and for checking in often. I'm so grateful to you.

To my publishing team: thanks for being patient, thorough, kind and totally accepting to take my lead on the PR that surrounded this book. You've all been ace to work with!

To Emma and Geoff: thanks for sharing with us your piece of paradise so that I can write these books and recharge. Every time I see you both I learn so much from you. You're both amazing. Thank you.

To Trevi, Kidscape, Women's Aid and Refuge: thank you for trusting me to represent your charities. Despite incessant attempts by the minority to undermine our relationships, you have all been so loyal to me and allowed me to campaign with you and shout about your work. I am honoured to support you.

To HMCTS – Carrie and team, the judges, the magistrates, the frightening man that taps at his computer and talks to the magistrates! – all of you . . . thank you for listening to little old me, for bringing me into your organisation as a critical friend to change the way we support domestic-abuse victims and survivors. I am so excited to be a part of this change.

To Wilby's preschool – Hannah and team – thank you for helping Josh and me navigate our way through some really dark days, for passing us the tissues in the meetings, for allowing us to 'feel' and for supporting us constantly. You have made our baby the happiest, most welcomed and loved little boy. I wish I could clone your education setting and incredible team and pop them around the world for children to have everywhere, because yours is honestly life-changing.

To all of you who have bought this book and who support me online, whether that's liking PTWM posts or shopping at the Patchwork store: all of you are the reason I am still here, still going and still having way more good days than bad. I love you all, thank you x